BACKYARD BIOLGY

Discover the Life Cycles and Adaptations Outside Your Door

with Hands-On Science Activities

Donna Latham
Illustrated by Michelle Simpson

Titles in the **Build It Yourself Accessible Science** Set

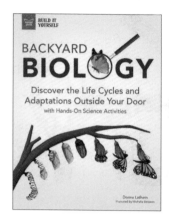

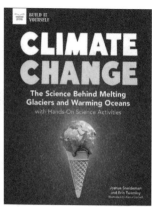

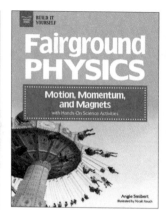

Check out more titles at www.nomadpress.net

Nomad Press

A division of Nomad Communications

10 9 8 7 6 5 4 3 2 1

This book was manufactured by Versa Press, East Peoria, Illinois
April 2020, Job #J19-12321
ISBN Softcover: 978-1-61930-895-4
ISBN Hardcover: 978-1-61930-892-3

Educational Consultant, Marla Conn

Questions regarding the ordering of this book should be addressed to
Nomad Press
2456 Christian St., White River Junction, VT 05001
www.nomadpress.net

Printed in the United States.

CONTENTS

Backyards Around the World . . . iv

Introduction
The Study of Life . . . 1

Chapter 1
Cells Alive! . . . 12

Chapter 2
Microbiology Reveals an Invisible World . . . 26

Chapter 3
Plants Make Life Possible . . . 44

Chapter 4
Plant Life Cycles . . . 57

Chapter 5
Adaptations Are a
Matter of Life and Death . . . 73

Chapter 6
Animal Life Cycles . . . 88

Chapter 7
Be the Difference . . . 98

Glossary • Metric Conversions
Resources • Essential Questions • Index

**Interested in
Primary Sources?
Look for this icon.** (PS)

Use a smartphone or tablet app to scan the QR code and explore more! Photos are also primary sources because a photograph takes a picture at the moment something happens. You can find a list of URLs on the Resources page. If the QR code doesn't work, try searching the internet with the Keyword Prompts to find other helpful sources.

🔎 biology

BACKYARDS AROUND THE WORLD

BACKYARD IN NORTH AMERICA

BACKYARD IN GREENLAND

BACKYARD IN SOUTH AMERICA

BACKYARD IN RUSSIA

BACKYARD IN NORWAY

BACKYARD IN JAPAN

BACKYARD IN GERMANY

THE STUDY OF
LIFE

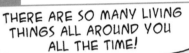

Where do you live? In the country, in a city, by the beach, near a desert? Wherever you are, you can find a whole lot of life right outside your door!

Life is everywhere. Life flourishes in deserts, forests, and oceans—even in the Arctic. You can find a place to explore living things almost anywhere you go. But even if you don't have plans to travel anytime soon, you can be a **biologist** in your own neighborhood.

Your community is an ideal place for scientific investigation. Parks, playgrounds, and nature preserves are outdoor science labs. Discover life over your head, under your toes, and at your fingertips. Ask questions, make predictions, and record your observations. Think like a scientist!

ESSENTIAL QUESTION

What characteristics do most living things share?

BACKYARD BIOLOGY

WORDS TO KNOW

biologist: a scientist who studies biology.

biology: the study of life and of living organisms.

diversity: a range of different things.

organism: any living thing.

ecosystem: a community of living and nonliving things and their environments.

microorganism: a living thing so small that it can be seen only with a microscope.

species: a group of plants or animals that are closely related and produce offspring.

predator: an animal that hunts another animal for food.

ichthyologist: a scientist who studies fish.

marine biology: the study of life in the water.

microbiology: the study of microorganisms.

botany: the study of plants.

zoology: the study of animals.

adapt: to change to survive in new or different conditions.

camouflage: the use of colors or patterns to blend in with a background.

adaptation: a change a plant or animal has made to help it survive.

LIFE ON EARTH

Biology is the study of life and living things. Earth boasts a mind-boggling **diversity** of **organisms** and **ecosystems**. Plus, all life on Earth is connected. Life forms range from invisible **microorganisms** squirming under your thumbnail to gigantic blue whales swimming in oceans.

Earth's **species** are so varied and plentiful, it's tricky to identify how many there are. According to the National Science Foundation, scientists have named and recorded 1.9 million species out of about 8.7 million species in existence. Scientists are always finding new species—some believe Earth's total number may be closer to 10 million.

For example, in 2018, a research team discovered an amazing, newly identified species in deep waters off the coast of Belize. While some people think the creature resembles an anime character, it's actually a big-eyed dogfish shark! About 20 to 28 inches in length, this slender shark is an aggressive **predator**. Scientists named the shark *Squalus clarkae*, or "Genie's dogfish" to honor Eugenie Clark (1922–2015), an American **ichthyologist** and **marine biology** pioneer. Earth added a new named species to its booming total number.

Take a look at *Squalus clarkae* in this video!

🔎 Florida Today Squalus clarkae

BOUNTIFUL BIOLOGY

Will you discover a new species? Maybe! As a backyard biologist, you'll explore three different branches of biology.

- **Microbiology** is the study of microorganisms. Micro means "small." Microorganisms are so tiny, they can't be seen with the human eye alone. To view them, people need microscopes.

- **Botany** is the study of plants. Plants are essential to the natural world. They help make life on Earth possible.

The prefix BIO means "LIFE." The suffix OLOGY means "THE STUDY OF."

- **Zoology** is the study of animals. Like plants, animals **adapt** to the world around them.

For example, the mossy leaf-tailed gecko **camouflages** against surrounding trees and rocks. It disappears as though it was wearing an invisibility cloak. Other animals develop behaviors and physical traits necessary for survival. What **adaptations** will you observe in your backyard adventures?

Can you spot the mossy leaf-tailed gecko in this photo?
Credit: Frank Vassen (CC BY 2.0)

3

WORDS TO KNOW

cell: the most basic part of a living thing. Billions of cells make up a plant or animal, while other organisms are single-celled.

reproduce: to make something new just like itself. To have babies.

environment: everything in nature, living and nonliving, including animals, plants, rocks, soil, and water.

life cycle: the growth and changes a living thing goes through, from birth to death.

regurgitate: to throw up partially digested food to feed a baby.

LIVING . . . OR NOT?

Microorganisms, plants, and animals are all living things. Take a look at your surroundings. What's alive? A friend sitting next to you? A pet snoozing in your lap? Perhaps a bright green wild parakeet chirps outside. Do you see a jackrabbit sniffing around a prickly pear cactus?

Peek around again. What are some nonliving things? What about this book or your tablet? Are you sitting at a desk or table? Using a laptop? Outside, you might see soil and rocks.

Living things on Earth can be wildly different from one another. Imagine a parakeet and the prickly pear cactus. They don't seem much alike, do they? A parakeet is an animal. A cactus is a plant. But both are alive.

Sometimes, it's tricky to tell the difference between living and nonliving things. How can you tell when something is alive? All living things share the following common characteristics.

- Living things are made up of one or more **cells**.

- Living things need energy to survive.

- Living things grow, develop, and die.

- Living things **reproduce**, or have babies.

- Living things respond to what's around them in their **environments**.

- Livings things adapt to survive in their environments.

The Largest Animal On Earth

What animal has a gargantuan heart the weight of a small car? And a monster tongue the weight of an elephant? The blue whale, the largest animal that has ever lived on Earth! Babies, called calves, measure about 23 feet at birth. Massive males grow to a whopping length of 82 feet. Females are even more gigantic. They rule the waves at 110 feet long.

A prickly pear cactus

Plus, every living thing has a **life cycle**. Living organisms are born. As they develop, they grow and change. They reproduce. In time, they die.

Consider a parakeet's life cycle. It grows in an egg laid by its mother. After pecking out of its shell, the tiny chick is very weak. The chick can hardly move its featherless body, and its mother needs to sit on it to keep it warm. She chews and swallows crunchy seeds, then **regurgitates** them right into her baby's beak. As days go by, the little chick grows stronger. It grows fluffy feathers. Within four weeks, the chick is as big as its mother. As an adult, the bird has babies of its own. Eventually, like all living things, the parakeet dies.

Of course, the **PARAKEET'S LIFE** wouldn't be **POSSIBLE** without one important factor: the **SUN**.

THANKS, SUN!

Without the sun, life on Earth couldn't exist. The sun is the source of most of the energy on Earth. It provides the planet's warmth and makes life possible. Plants need sunlight to grow. Without the sun, there would be no plants.

Without plants, the connected circle of life would wither and die. All land animals depend on plants for survival. You depend on plants, too. Plants provide food and oxygen. They are a crucial part of every ecosystem.

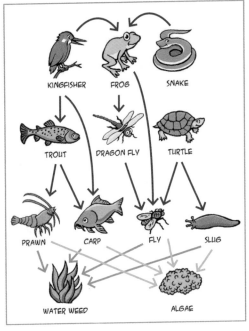
Food web

BACKYARD BIOLOGY

An ecosystem passes the sun's energy along to every member of its team. Microorganisms, plants, and animals mingle. Through **food chains**, they maintain a complex circle of life. All food chains, or flows of energy in ecosystems, begin with plants. A food web is several interconnected food chains.

Plants are **producers**. This means they make their own food. Since food chains start with producers, plants are critical. They form the food chain's foundation. Plants capture the sun's energy and pass it along to the animals that eat them.

Unlike plants, animals can't produce their own food. Animals are **consumers**, the next link in the chain. They are grouped depending on what they eat. The fight for survival means eat or be eaten! Some animals, such as the North American elk and the snowshoe hare, gobble plants. These **herbivores** eat crunchy nuts and seeds, nibble fruits and flowers, and chomp on leaves and stems.

These elk are herbivores.
Credit: James St. John (CC BY 2.0)

Carnivores, such as the great white shark and the great horned owl, are predators that eat other animals. Torpedo-shaped with cavernous jaws, great whites ambush **prey**. They gorge on sea lions, small whales, and other sharks. Great horned owls are sneaky night hunters snacking on shrews, meadow voles, and raccoons. They devour other birds, including ducks and geese.

But **omnivores** aren't fussy! These animals, such as cockroaches and wild pond turtles, eat both plants and animals. Are you an omnivore?

We'll take a look at many different food webs in this book.

Decomposers Are Rotten!

The circle of life includes death. **Decomposers** are a vital link in the food chain. Decomposers include ants, worms, and **fungi**. They do an ecosystem's dirty work, breaking down dead plants and animals so they rot. Decomposers decay chunks of dead wood. They even feast on animal wastes. They're nature's recyclers because they pass **nutrients** back into the soil to keep it **fertile**. The circle of life rolls on and on.

glacier: an enormous mass of frozen snow and ice that moves across the earth's surface.

drought: a long period of unusually low rainfall that can harm plants and animals.

climate change: the long-term change in temperature and weather patterns across a large area, in particular a change apparent from the mid-to-late twentieth century onward that has been strongly attributed to the use of fossil fuels as an energy source.

wildlife: animals, birds, and other things that live wild in nature.

fossil fuel: a fuel made from the remains of plants and animals that lived millions of years ago. Coal, oil, and natural gas are fossil fuels.

BE A NATURE DETECTIVE

Detectives use special tools of the trade to track down clues and solve mysteries. Assemble your own toolkit to scout for nature clues. Stash your supplies in a backpack and hang it in the same place all the time, so it's always ready and waiting.

Here are some things to keep in your kit:

- Binoculars to study things that are far away

- A magnifying glass for zooming in close

- A small garden shovel and some old spoons for collecting soil samples

- Recycled plastic containers with lids to store samples

- Science journal and pencils

Climate Change Corner

Melting **glaciers**. Raging wildfires. Torrential downpours. Severe **droughts**. **Climate change** is not only evident in Earth's rising temperatures. It's everywhere—even in your own backyard. Climate change impacts people, their homes, and their ways of earning a living. It threatens the environment, endangers **wildlife**, and shrivels freshwater supplies. Nearly all scientists agree climate change is caused by human activities, such as chopping down forests and burning **fossil fuels**. Around the world, leaders are joining together to explore ways we can halt global warming. They discuss ways to stem the tides of warmer, rising waters and halt catastrophic consequences—consequences we can prevent through action. Throughout this book, we'll explore ways of being good stewards of planet Earth and taking steps to protect our home.

LIVING THINGS also need nonliving things to stay alive. **NONLIVING** things include air, rocks, soil, and water. Every part of an **ECOSYSTEM** is part of a team. Each player interacts with all the other players in the environment. Team Nature keeps the whole system **BALANCED** and **THRIVING**.

This book is full of projects and activities that tap into your curiosity about the living world. Most projects involve ecosystems outside your door—whether right in your own backyard, in a neighborhood park or playground, or in a nature preserve.

Discover why cells are called life's building blocks and explore the invisible world of microorganisms. Learn about life cycles of a diverse world of plants and animals. And you'll explore climate change, learn about environmental threats to the planet, and find ways you can help.

Of course, you already know safety's first. Ask an adult for help when handling materials such as raw eggs and rubbing alcohol. Don't use the oven or sharp objects by yourself. Pay attention to safety warnings at the beginning of some projects. Before you explore outside, team up with an adult to identify and list all the safety rules you will follow.

Leaves of three? Let 'em be!

This old rhyme warns against poison ivy and poison oak. When touched, these poisonous plants trigger allergic reactions. They cause splotchy rashes, terrible itching, and blisters. Head to the library to learn about poisonous plants that grow in your area. Find out what they look like so you can identify and avoid touching these plants.

Exploring outdoors is a fantastic opportunity for discovery. And it's a chance to pitch in and protect the planet. Respect nature as you explore it by treating it gently. Try to avoid actions that could cause any harm. Practice the method of carry in, carry out. This means that whatever you take with you when you go exploring, you need to take away with you when you leave.

Ready to get started? Let's go!

Good Science Practices

Every good scientist keeps a science journal!

Scientists use the scientific method to keep their experiments organized. Choose a notebook to use as your science journal. As you read through this book and do the activities, keep track of your observations and record each step in a scientific method worksheet, like the one shown here.

Question: What are we trying to find out? What problem are we trying to solve?

Research: What is already known about the problem?

Hypothesis/Prediction: What do we think the answer will be?

Equipment: What supplies are we using?

Method: What procedure are we following?

Results: What happened? Why?

Each chapter of this book begins with an essential question to help guide your exploration of the biology around you. Keep the question in your mind as you read the chapter. At the end of each chapter, use your science journal to record your thoughts and answers.

ESSENTIAL QUESTION

What characteristics do most living things share?

PLANT A MYSTERY
GREENHOUSE GARDEN

BIO BOX
- garden gloves
- trowel
- sealable bags
- generous soil samples from three different sites
- shoebox lid
- plastic wrap
- toothpicks
- sticky notes

What might be lurking in the soil? Find out by taking samples of soil from three different sites and seeing what grows!

▶ **Select three sites for collecting samples.** You might choose your backyard, a playground, a field, a nature preserve, or a beach. At each site, wear garden gloves as you collect soil with a trowel and pour it into a sealable bag. Label the bag so you know where this sample came from.

▶ **Line the inside of a shoebox lid with plastic wrap** to make a waterproof bottom for your greenhouse. With a marker, divide the lid into three equal horizontal sections.

▶ **Make three garden stakes with toothpicks and sticky notes.** On each sticky note, write the name of one field site. Carefully poke a toothpick through the sticky note to make a little flag. Set stakes aside for now.

▶ **Pour the first sample into its section of the lid.** Use a magnifying glass to examine the sample. What color is it? Is it moist, dry, sandy? Do you see any seeds? Any roots or shoots? Press the identifying toothpick stake into the soil. Repeat with the second and third samples. Start a scientific method worksheet in your science journal. Record your observations and predict what plants will sprout.

▶ **Lightly water, but don't flood, the samples.** With another sheet of plastic wrap, create a puffy roof for the greenhouse. Tape it securely in place. Place the greenhouse in a sunny location.

▶ **How long does it take plants to sprout?** Are plants different or the same among the samples? Can you identify any? Record your observations in your science journal.

Consider This

What do the different plants tell you about the soil and where it came from? Can you identify any plants that like to grow near water or in the shade?

Chapter 1

CELLS
ALIVE!

Cells keep organisms alive! Cells are living things. They are the smallest, most basic units of all life. Every living thing is made of cells: from microorganisms such as bacteria and amoebae wriggling in pond scum to a ravenous alligator cruising a swamp, from a Venus flytrap to the tiny frog it snares, from a snow leopard to the bits of moss under its paws. And you!

There are many different kinds of cells. That's why the alligator looks different from a Venus flytrap. Even in your own body, skin cells are different from the cells that make up your lungs. As different as cells are, however, they all perform many of the same functions and have many of the same basic parts. Let's take a look, starting with very simple organisms made of just one cell.

ESSENTIAL QUESTION

How do cells act as life's building blocks?

ONE-CELLED WONDERS

Some organisms, such as amoebae, are made of only one cell. Single-celled life forms are called **unicellular**. They are smaller in size and simpler than living things made of many cells. You can't see them with the naked eye. But they're all around you!

Where do amoebae live? They're in the puddles you leap over and in the mucky soil that squishes under your sneakers. Jelly-like amoebae thrive inside some animals. They supply nibbles of food for water fleas and mussels. When they invade people's bodies, some amoebae can cause harmful illnesses.

Amoebae don't have any hard parts. Made of a glob of colorless liquid called **protoplasm**, these one-celled wonders constantly change shape to eat and move.

WORDS TO KNOW

bacteria: single-celled organisms found in soil, water, plants, and animals. They help decay food. Some bacteria are harmful. Singular is bacterium.

amoebae: bloblike, single-celled organisms. Singular is amoeba.

unicellular: made of only one cell.

protoplasm: the colorless liquid that forms the living matter of a cell.

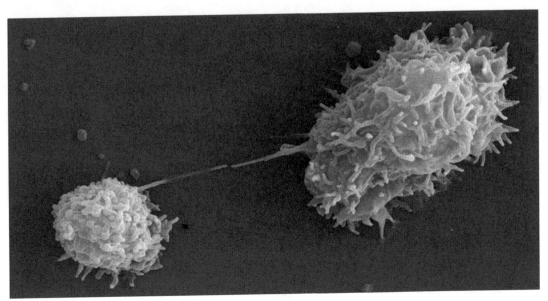

Two single-celled organisms

BACKYARD BIOLOGY

How does a microscopic blob of jelly get around? With a **pseudopod**, or false foot! A slimy amoeba forms flowing, foot-like bulges out of **cytoplasm**. With these pseudopods, the amoeba drags itself to a different location.

Watch this amazing video that captures an amoeba's locomotion, or movement. How does the blobby amoeba use pseudopods to crawl?

🔎 CR King crawling amoeba

PS

Because the amoeba has no teeth or even a mouth, eating looks a lot different from what you usually see at the dinner table. Imagine an amoeba floating in pond scum. A yummy bacterium floats close by. The amoeba oozes toward its lunch. It stretches out pseudopods and surrounds its prey. Once the bacterium is surrounded and trapped, the amoeba **digests** it.

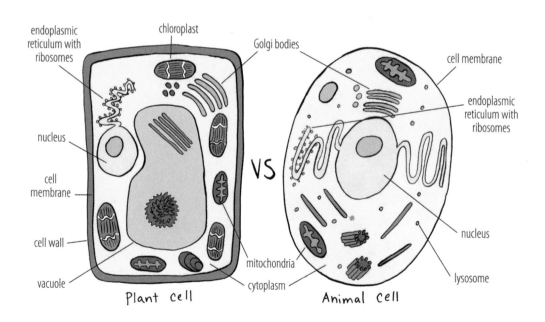

Climate Change Corner

Do you live in an area impacted by **algae blooms**? Climate change and the warming of the planet make out-of-control algae blooms occur more frequently. **Toxic** blue-green **algae** are actually bacteria. Called **cyanobacteria**, they can cause health issues, such as skin and eye irritations, for people who accidentally touch the algae. Cyanobacteria can prove **fatal** to dogs that take a dip in scum and lap it up. The toxic algae also slime sand and kill fish. Plus, they stink! Some folks say they reek of moldy bread. Sometimes, a toxic algae bloom really takes over. Lake Okeechobee in Florida boasts a surface area of 730 square miles. The Sunshine State's largest freshwater lake meanders through miles of coastland and draws about 6 million visitors annually. In 2018, toxic algae covered 90 percent of the water! What caused the historically huge bloom? Richard P. Stumpf, an oceanographer with the National Oceanic and Atmospheric Administration (NOAA), spoke to *The New York Times*. Stumpf explained that rain, hot weather, and a heavy build-up of phosphorus and nitrogen from **fertilizers** used on farms launched the bloom.

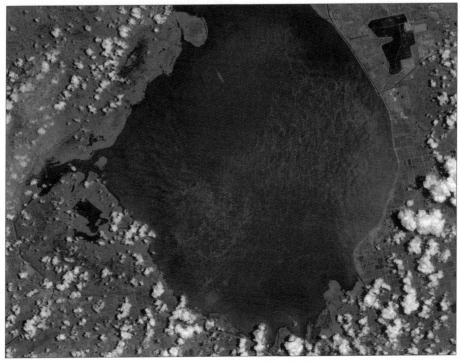

An aerial view of Lake Okeechobee

Credit: NASA

WORDS TO KNOW

fission: the splitting of a single-celled organism into two parts.

asexual: reproduction without male and female cells joining.

multicellular: made up of many cells.

tissue: a group or mass of similar cells working together to perform common functions in plants and animals.

organ: a body part that has a certain function, such as the heart or kidneys.

organ system: a group of organs in a living body that work together to do a specific job.

organelle: a structure inside a cell that performs a special function or job.

nucleus: the central part of a cell.

mitochondria: the parts of a cell that change food into energy.

ribosome: the protein builder in a cell.

Golgi bodies: sacs that receive proteins from the cell, put them together with other proteins, and send them around the cell.

endoplasmic reticulum: a network of membranes that makes changes and transports materials through a cell.

lysosome: an organelle that aids in digestion.

An amoeba reproduces in a process called **fission**. It's an **asexual** process. To reproduce, an amoeba stops moving and splits into two equal parts. It makes an identical copy of itself and the copy becomes a new amoeba.

MULTICELLULAR ORGANISMS GET ORGANIZED!

Most organisms, including people, other animals, and plants, are made of many cells. They are **multicellular**. These organisms are larger and more complex than unicellular organisms. Multicellular living things contain specialized cells that work together to do a job. For example, red blood cells carry oxygen through your body. Other cells might be specific to your heart.

Cells of the same type cluster to form **tissues**. These tissues group together to create **organs**. Two or more different organs may form an **organ system**. In this way, specialized cells form tissues, organs, and organ systems that function together. Each cell has a specific job to perform, and all cells must work together to keep you alive and healthy.

It takes only a pinkie to count the number of cells in an AMOEBA. But you'd probably lose count if you tried to count the CELLS in your own body. It's bursting with about 37.2 TRILLION CELLS!

It's hard to imagine that tiny cells have even tinier parts inside them. These **organelles**, which means "little organs," carry out certain functions. They all pitch in to tend to the cell's needs. Organelles help the cell take in air and food. They kick out wastes. These teeny organs have huge jobs to tackle.

How did scientists estimate the total number of cells in the human body? It was a challenge! **Read this article to explore the process.**

Smithsonian 37.2 trillion cells

Although plant and animal cells are different, they have some organelles in common. Both plant and animal cells contain a large, round **nucleus**. The nucleus is the big boss, like the cell's control tower or brain. The nucleus gives orders to the cell, such as when to grow and when to reproduce.

Cells are filled with rubbery, sticky cytoplasm. Cytoplasm provides the cell with shape and holds organelles in a gooey grip. Inside cytoplasm, tube-shaped **mitochondria** are in charge of changing food into energy. Other organelles include **ribosomes**, **Golgi bodies**, and **endoplasmic reticulum**. These are also essential, while **lysosomes** in animal cells work to break down and digest food.

BACKYARD BIOLOGY

WORDS TO KNOW

proteins: substances found in all plants and animals that provide the major structural and functional components of cells.

chloroplast: the part of a plant cell in which sunlight is converted to energy.

pigment: a substance that gives something its color.

chlorophyll: the chemical in a plant's cell that gives a plant its green color.

vacuole: a compartment in the cytoplasm of a plant cell that stores food and waste.

membrane: the outer layer of a cell that allows materials to pass in and out.

cell wall: the part of a plant cell that gives shape to the cell.

Ribosomes perform like miniature machines in charge of building **proteins**, called protein synthesis. They can be free-floating in the cytoplasm or attached to endoplasmic reticulum.

Endoplasmic reticulum are a network of membranes that move proteins to the Golgi bodies. The Golgi bodies, which are larger than other cell components, are like sacks. They receive proteins, sort them, and assemble them with other proteins. Then, they move the proteins through the cell.

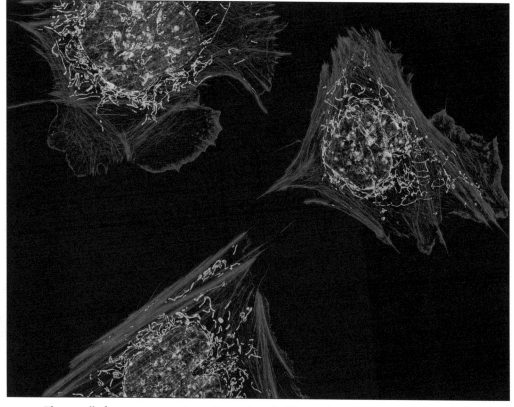

These cells from a mouse show the nucleus in blue and the mitochondria in green.
Credit: NICHD (CC BY 2.0)

How Are Plant Cells Different?

Most green plants are food factories. They produce their own food. Special cells get the job done. **Chloroplasts** are in charge of converting the sun's energy into stored energy. Chloroplasts contain green **pigment** called **chlorophyll**. Chlorophyll does more than make plants a beautiful green color. It also works as a microscopic solar panel that snags sunlight needed to churn out food. All plant cells contain a **vacuole**—a bag of fluid floating in cytoplasm. The vacuole is the cell's warehouse. It stores pigment, food, and wastes.

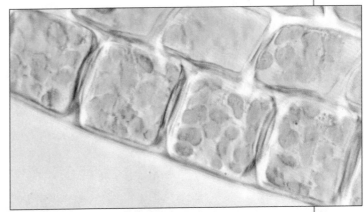

Microscopic moss chloroplasts
Credit: Kelvinsong (CC BY 3.0)

Located in every organism on Earth, proteins are essential for life. Cells must make proteins for growth, health, and repair. Cells require proteins for shape and structure.

A **membrane** surrounds a cell in a layer like a teeny, sealable bag. In a plant cell, membranes are held inside a rigid **cell wall** that gives shape to cells. In an animal cell, the membrane is stretchy. In both, the membrane is a gatekeeper. It allows nutrients in and lets wastes out.

Some of the most fascinating life forms are the ones we can't even see! We'll learn more about them in the next chapter.

ESSENTIAL QUESTION

How do cells act as life's building blocks?

YEAST BALLOON
BLOW UP

Yeast is a single-celled fungus. Shake a few grains of baker's yeast into your palm and check them out. The yeast grains may not seem to be alive, but they are just **dormant** right now. Let's see what happens when you activate a yeast culture. Can you inflate a balloon with it?

> **Hint:** Don't use hot water. That kills yeast.

> **Pour the baker's yeast into the bottle.** Carefully pour very warm tap water, about 110 degrees Fahrenheit (43 degrees Celsius), into the bottle until it's about one-quarter full. Swirl the bottle in a circular motion to dissolve the yeast. As yeast is absorbed in water, it becomes active. Yeast cells are **microscopic**, so you won't be able to see any signs of life.

> **Add 2 tablespoons of sugar to the bottle to feed the yeast.** Yeast uses sugar's energy to become more active. Swirl the bottle again to dissolve the sugar. How is the yeast changing? Is it bubbly or foamy?

> **Fill the bottle with more very warm water**—all the way to the top of the neck.

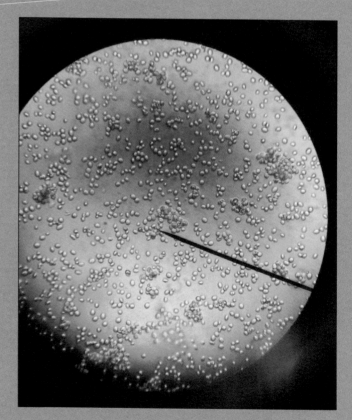

Yeast under a microscope
Credit: Sam LaRussa (CC BY 2.0)

WORDS TO KNOW

dormant: in a state of rest or inactivity.

microscopic: something so small it can be seen only under a microscope.

incubate: to develop.

fermentation: a chemical reaction that breaks down food.

Egyptologist: a person who studies the history and culture of ancient Egypt.

Stretch a small balloon to loosen it. Blow it up several times. Check to make sure the balloon has no leaks. Then, deflate it. Slip the deflated balloon over the bottle's neck.

In your science journal, make a scientific method worksheet to record your predictions and results. Then, **incubate** your yeast culture in a warm location away from drafts. After a few hours, check your experiment. What is happening? It may take longer, depending on your environment.

Try This!

Yeast in action! Watch a time-lapse film of yeast growing. What do you notice about the ways it foams and bubbles as it changes? What else do you observe?

🔎 yeast growth time lapse

WHAT'S HAPPENING?

As yeast gobbles sugar, it releases the gas carbon dioxide (CO_2). It releases more and more gas, which bubbles in the bottle. Yeast also makes more yeast. As more and more gas is produced, the gas has to go somewhere: into the balloon!

#AncientBaking

Have you ever used yeast to bake bread? Though a lowly, single-celled fungus, yeast is the powerhouse behind **fermentation**. That's the process that causes dough to rise. Some evidence suggests ancient Egyptians used yeast in baking.

You might recognize physicist and video game developer Seamus Blackley as the "father of the Xbox." Multitalented Blackley is also an amateur **Egyptologist** and a baking enthusiast. Blackley teamed with Dr. Serena Love, an Egyptologist, and Richard Bowman, a microbiologist. The trio collected samples of 4,500-year-old dormant yeast from ancient Egyptian pots. Blackley activated the ancient samples—and baked bread with them! Read this thread from his Twitter feed to discover how he did it and how the bread turned out.

🔎 Seamus Blackley twitter

EDIBLE
CELL MODEL

Follow the recipe to create an edible cell. Kiwi, tangerines, berries, and more represent an animal cell's organelles. Light-colored gelatin allows organelles to stand out so you can easily see them. After the gelatin sets, spoon up a jiggly treat!

Be Careful: Wash your hands before handling food items. Ask an adult to help you with boiling water.

❯ **Follow the directions on the gelatin package to prepare the mix,** but use only half the amounts of boiling and cold water indicated on the package. Less water creates a firmer base for edible organelles.

❯ **Allow the gelatin to cool to room temperature.** Use a large, empty Ziploc bag to represent the cell membrane. Carefully place it inside a saucepan. Ask an adult to help you pour the cooled gelatin, which represents cytoplasm, into the bag. Fill it about one-third full.

❯ **Add organelles by arranging fruit to represent the nucleus,** mitochondria, lysosomes, and ribosomes. Add ribbon candy to represent Golgi bodies. Press the ends of the fruit strips together to form a single long strip. Fold it back and forth in a fanned fashion to resemble wavy endoplasmic reticulum.

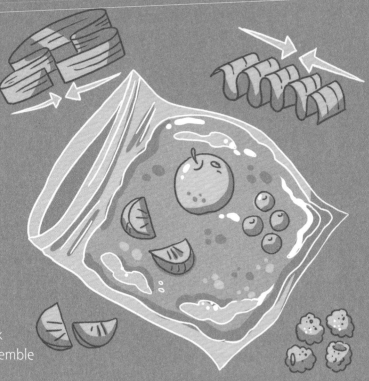

On the Move!

In the early nineteenth century, French physiologist Henri Dutrochet (1776–1847) observed materials moving in and out of cells through the membrane. He called this method of transportation osmosis. Some molecules move across the membrane freely, while others need help from protein transporters. **Molecules** move within the cell, too, where it can get crowded. They move from areas where there are lots of molecules to an area where there are fewer molecules. This is known as diffusion. Another important movement that takes place in cells involves messenger RNA (mRNA), which is used by the cell to let the ribosomes know what kind of protein is needed. Whole cells can move as well—they look as though they are crawling! Some cells have tiny hairs called cilia around the outside that help the cell move. Other cells might have what's called a flagella, which is more like a tail. There are fewer flagella, but they're longer than the cilia. They work like the kick of a swim stroke to push the cell along.

> **Carefully squeeze the air out of the bag.** Tightly seal it. Lay the bag flat on a cookie sheet. Gently move the fruit around so the organelles aren't bunched together.

> **Place the cookie sheet in the refrigerator so the gelatin can set.** Wait at least an hour, then check periodically. Gently touch the bag to check progress. The gelatin may take a few hours to set firmly.

> **After the gelatin sets,** remove the cookie sheet from the refrigerator. In your science journal, sketch a diagram of the cell and label each component.

> **Carefully squeeze the cell into a dish.** Dig in and enjoy!

Try This!

Scientists use models to help them understand things. Make another cell model using nonedible items. What might you use for the cytoplasm? Nucleus? How does this model compare to your edible one?

WORDS TO KNOW

molecules: the tiny particles that make up everything.

BAGS O' BREAD
MOLD

Fungi lack chlorophyll. They can't obtain energy from the sun and can't produce their own food. To get energy, many fungi feast on dead organisms. Mold is a fuzzy, multicellular fungus that flourishes in many environments. It reproduces with **spores.** You can grow your own mold on slices of bread. What happens when you place the slices in different environments?

Caution: Some people are allergic to mold spores. Inhaling spores can be harmful. Keep plastic bags tightly sealed at all times. Don't touch mold. Ask an adult to help you choose environments out of reach of family members and pets. After you finish the project, ask an adult to safely dispose of your sealed bags.

❯ **Label two resealable sandwich bags with a permanent marker.** Write "Bright" on one and "Dark" on the other. Add the date to each.

❯ **Rub two cotton swabs against a floorboard,** table leg, or other dusty surface to collect samples. Be sure to rub both swabs in the same location. Then, brush one dusty swab over the surface of one slice of bread. Brush the second swab on another slice.

MOLDS grow in a variety of colors, from bright fluorescent **purple to drab olive green and rusty brown.**

❯ **Fill an eye dropper with water.** Drip 5 drops onto each slice of bread. Place one slice into the bright sandwich bag and the other into the dark bag. Seal the bags tightly.

Explore "Molds on Foods: Are They Dangerous?" published by USDA's Food Safety and Inspection Services.

🔎 USDA mold dangerous

❯ **For the bright bag,** choose a brightly lit, warm location such as a sunny windowsill. Choose a cool, dark location such as a basement for the dark bag. Let the mold spores incubate for a full week.

WORDS TO KNOW

spore: a structure produced by fungi that sprouts and grows into a new fungus.

> Make a scientific method worksheet in your science journal. What do you think will happen to the bread after a week? Which location is better for mold to flourish? Write down your hypothesis.

> After two days, gather the bags. Use a magnifying glass to examine your samples. Do you observe any mold, or is it still invisible? Note observations on your scientific method worksheet. Sketch and color illustrations of the samples. Then, return the bags to their locations.

> After five more days, gather the bags. Use the magnifying glass to examine your mold colonies. What do the samples look like now? Record your observations and make colored sketches. How do the samples compare? Were your predictions accurate?

Try This!

Mold can cause rashes, allergic reactions, and respiratory troubles. With family or friends, investigate foodborne molds and what you should do with food that's become moldy.

Moldy Medical Discovery: Penicillin

In September 1928, an oddball incident revolutionized medicine and impacted human history.

Scientist Alexander Fleming (1881–1955) arrived at work in his cluttered lab at St. Mary's Hospital in London, England. Before vacationing in his native Scotland, he had been growing colonies of *Staphylococcus aureus*, infectious bacteria, in uncovered petri dishes. After his return, Fleming spotted a weird, blue-green growth in the dishes. It contaminated the bacteria colonies. What was the strange invader? Mold!

The mysterious mold had wafted in the air from another lab and settled in the cultures. It left a clear ring around the bacteria. Fleming examined petri dishes under a microscope and observed that the mystery mold actually halted bacterial growth. He identified the mold as part of the *Penicillium* genus and dubbed its active agent "penicillin." Fleming realized his discovery might be used to treat infectious diseases.

By the 1940s, scientists developed an antibiotic from the same type of mold. In March 1942, Anne Miller of Connecticut nearly died from a blood infection. She became the first civilian to be treated with penicillin. It saved her life, and she made medical history.

Since its discovery, the antibiotic has cured more than 200 million people around the globe of infectious diseases.

Chapter 2

MICROBIOLOGY
REVEALS AN INVISIBLE WORLD

Did you know you're an ecosystem for life forms you can't even see? Wherever you go, an invisible world goes with you! Trillions of microorganisms, some good and some bad, hitch a ride on the surface of and inside your body. For microorganisms, your scalp is a thick jungle in which to roam, one eyelash a towering tree on which to perch. The tip of your fingernail is an exciting cliff.

Harmful microorganisms squirm behind your teeth and cause decay. Helpful microorganisms squiggle in your gut to help digest food. They churn lunch into nutrients, which your cells use for growth and fuel. Most of your body's invisible inhabitants are bacteria, one of Earth's smallest life forms.

ESSENTIAL QUESTION

How do tiny organisms impact our lives?

One way you can view microorganisms is by looking at them under light microscopes. With these microscopes, light passes through a slide. As you peer into the eyepiece, the scope displays a magnified image of a **specimen** right under your eye!

Microscopes reveal an unknown world. But it wasn't until the 1600s that scientists even became aware of microscopic cells. Scientists often build on the discoveries of other scientists, and Robert Hooke's (1635–1703) first microscopes inspired Antoni van Leeuwenhoek (1632–1723) toward an explosion of curiosity and discovery. Together, these two scientists **revolutionized** biology.

MICROBES are teeny, but their impact is enormous. Just how many species live on Earth? Scientists predict the total is a whopping **1 TRILLION.** That's 18 zeroes!

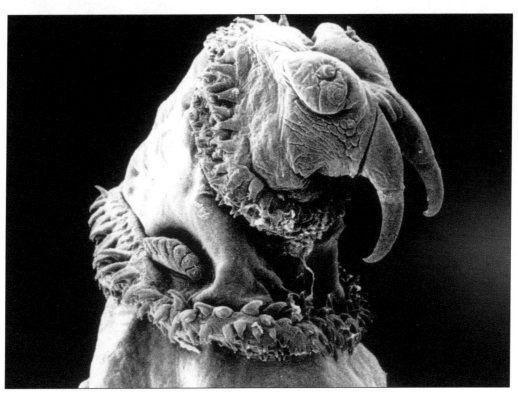

Take a look at a screw worm fly larva through an electron microscope!
Credit: Entomology, CSIRO (CC BY 3.0)

WORDS TO KNOW

compound microscope: a microscope with two or more lenses.

pioneer: to be one of the first to discover something new.

protozoa: microscopic, one-celled organisms. Singular is protozoon.

indigenous: native people who originally settled a region; also known as First Nation or First Peoples.

Inupiaq: a group of Alaska Natives whose territory spreads from Norton Sound on the Bering Sea to northern areas of the U.S.-Canada border. They are members of the larger Inuit culture.

FOUNDERS OF MICROBIOLOGY

Robert Hooke was an English physicist who experimented with early versions of microscopes and made drawings of what he saw when he looked through his rough **compound microscope**. He compiled his drawings and observations in a book called *Micrographia*. The book gave people the first glimpse into the microscopic world and changed people's ideas of life forever.

Hooke's drawings inspired Antoni van Leeuwenhoek, a fabric merchant from Holland, to build his own microscopes. He wanted to see some of these marvels for himself. Leeuwenhoek ground glass and hand-crafted small, simple, hand-held scopes. With his love of nature, sense of wonder, and endless curiosity, Leeuwenhoek became a **pioneer** in microbiology. He was the first to discover and describe **protozoa** and bacteria.

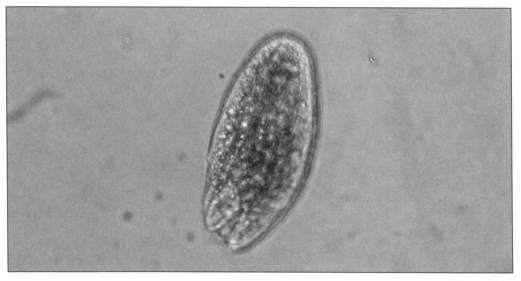

A protozoon
Credit: Donald Hobern (CC BY 2.0)

Microbiologist Dr. Kat Napaaqtuk Milligan-Myhre

Dr. Kat Napaaqtuk Milligan-Myhre is a microbiologist and assistant professor of biological studies at the University of Alaska Anchorage. An **indigenous Inupiaq**, Dr. Milligan-Myhre has worked in research for more than 20 years. A STEM advocate, she studies host-microbe interactions with a focus on marine organisms.

In a "#STEMStories" feature, Dr. Milligan-Myhre explained her research to the *Geeky Girl Realities* blog. "In my research, I use a fish found all over the northern hemisphere called threespine stickleback to study host-microbe interactions, and specifically how our genes influence how our gut microbes interact with our bodies. . . . I'm interested in how trillions of microbes in our gut help us grow, and how our gut microbes stop microbes that can cause disease from causing disease, and why that is different in one person vs. another person."

Threespine stickleback fish
Credit: Ryan Hagerty, U.S. Fish and Wildlife Service

When Dr. Milligan-Myhre collects sticklebacks in the field, she pauses to observe the fish and reflect. She wonders how microbes in sticklebacks' guts impact growth and behavior. Back in her university lab to conduct experiments, Dr. Milligan-Myhre works with about 15 students. She loves watching them grow as scientists.

In 1674, the curious merchant wondered about the lake near his home. During cold months, the lake sparkled with clear water. But Leeuwenhoek noticed that during the heat of summer, the water turned murky green.

Leeuwenhoek scooped a slimy sample of green water into a glass tube. He examined a drop of the liquid under a homemade lens he held up to his eye.

You can see some of Hooke's work at this website. Can you imagine what it must have felt like to view microscopic organisms for the first time?

🔎 Hunt Botanical Hooke

BACKYARD BIOLOGY

WORDS TO KNOW

microbiome: a community of microorganisms.

dust mite: a microscopic insect that feeds on dead skin cells. Dust mites are a common cause of allergies.

plaque: a sticky substance that forms on teeth and gums and causes decay.

sperm: the cell that comes from a male in the reproductive process.

View eye-popping images in this video! Can you guess what you are seeing before the identifying labels are displayed?

🔎 Spoof electron pics

PS

What he saw were hundreds of green flashes squirming and wriggling around! Leeuwenhoek marveled at these miniature swimming creatures.

He'd uncovered a **microbiome** that no one had seen before! He wrote about "very many little animalcules" whose movement "in the water was so fast and so random, upwards, downwards, and round in all directions that it was truly wonderful to see." Today, we call his animalcules "microorganisms."

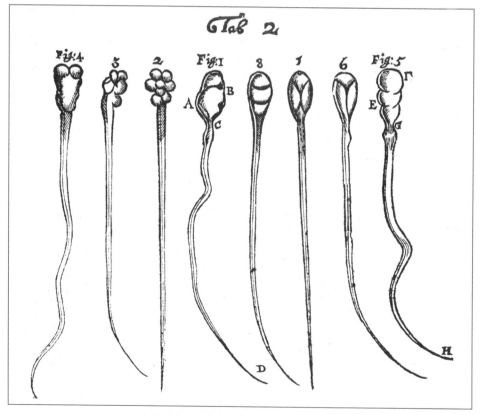

Credit: Wellcome Collection gallery (2018-04-03) (CC BY 4.0)

Do you have DUST BUNNIES under your bed?
Those are partly flakes of your own skin!
Your **SKIN'S** top layer is comprised of **DEAD CELLS**.
Every day, some of these cells flake off your body
and flutter to the floor. They mingle with human and
pet hair, dust, lint, and cobwebs and form a hairy,
clumpy **TUMBLEWEED.** As they roll around, dead cells
provide an all-you-can-eat feast for invisible **dust mites**.

WHAT?! DUST BUNNIES ARE ACTUALLY DEAD CELLS!

IT'S COMPLETELY NATURAL, ALL LIVING THINGS HAVE TO DIE AND GO SOMEWHERE.

IN THIS CASE, DUST MITES EAT THEM. IT'S JUST THE CIRCLE OF LIFE ON A SMALLER SCALE.

DUST MITES ARE KIND OF LIKE THE SCAVENGERS OF THE UNSEEN WORLD.

BUT WHY DID THEY CALL THEM DUST BUNNIES THEN? A CLUMP OF DEAD CELLS AND DIRT DOESN'T DESERVE A CUTE NAME LIKE THAT!

Leeuwenhoek became curious about what might be living inside us. Luckily, he knew two men who had never cleaned their teeth in their entire lives. Yuck! After bravely scraping off **plaque** samples, he put them under a microscope.

He saw "an unbelievably great company of living animalcules." He said they were "a-swimming more nimbly than any I had ever seen up to this time. . . ." Before Leeuwenhoek's discoveries, no one imagined there were billions and billions of tiny creatures living right under (and even in!) our noses. Leeuwenhoek also discovered blood cells and was the first person to view living **sperm** cells from animals.

immunization: making a person or animal immune to infectious disease.

infectious: able to spread quickly from one person to others.

vaccine: a substance made up of dead or weakened organisms that, when injected, causes an animal to produce antibodies that protect from the disease caused by those organisms.

immune system: the system that protects the body against disease and infection.

antibodies: proteins that help the immune system fight infections or bacteria.

probiotics: microorganisms consumed in foods such as yogurt or miso to keep healthy bacteria in the digestive tract.

virologist: a scientist who studies viruses.

virus: a non-living microbe that can cause disease. It can only spread inside the living cells of an organism.

MICROBIOLOGY AND VACCINES

In the last chapter you read about Alexander Fleming's oddball discovery of penicillin. From early pioneers in microbiology to Fleming's experiments to today's discoveries, advances impact scientific knowledge of diseases and their treatments. Advances benefit not only people but also animals and make enormous contributions to global health.

Chickenpox. Smallpox. Polio. Whooping cough. Measles, mumps, and rubella. **Immunizations** provide people with protection from these **infectious** diseases. For more than two centuries, human health has benefited from **vaccines**. Microbiologists developed vaccines that use weakened, disease-causing microorganisms. Vaccines stimulate the human body's **immune system**. The body responds to the invader as if it's under attack. It produces **antibodies** and goes to battle. It wipes out the invader and learns to do the same if confronted with the same microorganism in the future.

Consider two revolutionary contributions to world health, which occurred about 160 years apart. English doctor and scientist Edward Jenner (1749–1823) is dubbed "The Father of Immunology."

Not all **BACTERIA** are bad for you. Have you ever eaten yogurt, kefir, kimchee, or miso? Those foods contain healthy bacteria called **probiotics**. **PROBIOTICS** help you digest food and keep your immune system strong so you can fight germs. When the label on a yogurt container states it has live and active cultures, it means it has probiotics.

He introduced the smallpox vaccine in 1796, the first vaccination used to prevent the deadly airborne disease, which causes flu-like symptoms and blisters filled with pus. By 1977, the disease was totally wiped out. In 1955, medical research and **virologist** Jonas Salk (1914–1995) developed the polio vaccination to combat the polio **virus**. The disease caused paralysis, and many who contracted it where children. By 1979, the disease had been eradicated in the United States.

DOGS AND CATS are beloved members of our families. **FERRETS** are, too. In some states, laws require that these pets be **VACCINATED** for rabies.

Try This!

Check out St. Louis Community College's site, Highlights in the History of Microbiology. Then, research smallpox, polio, and other diseases to learn their symptoms, the way they spread, and their impact on human health throughout history. Share your findings with friends or family.

St. Louis Community College Microbiology

Nature Detective

Fungi are important decomposers. For energy, fungi feast on dead plants, dead animals, and poop. Fungi suck away water and nutrients from dead organisms, causing them to rot. Mushrooms are one type of fungus. They love cool, dark, moist environments. They grow quickly in clumps and even sprout overnight. After a heavy rainfall, scout outdoors for mushrooms. Search under logs, around tree stumps, and in mounds of decomposing leaves. Sketch what you discover or snap photos. Use online and library resources to identify different fungi. Remember, some wild mushrooms are poisonous, so don't touch or taste any! Even touching might result in skin irritations.

antibiotic overuse: using antibiotics when not needed.

electron microscope: a type of microscope that uses a beam of electrons to create an image of the specimen.

resistant bacteria: bacteria that cannot be killed with antibiotics.

bacteriologist: a scientist who studies bacteria.

ANTIBIOTIC OVERUSE

Have you taken antibiotics? You've read that penicillin revolutionized medicine. It helped millions across the world. Today, there are more than 100 different types of antibiotics. Doctors prescribe them to treat infections. But what happens when antibiotics are prescribed too much or otherwise misused?

Antibiotic overuse is using antibiotics when they are not needed. When antibiotics are incorrectly used, germs become resistant. **Resistant bacteria** don't respond. Sometimes, they mutate. They transform into bacteria that's even more difficult to treat.

How do antibiotics get overprescribed? Sometimes, doctors must wait for a patient's lab results before they know if an infection is caused by bacteria or a virus. Only bacteria respond to antibiotics. Viruses don't.

Today's electron microscopes provide greater MAGNIFICATION than light microscopes. Instead of light, they use a beam of electrons as a source of illumination to create an image for viewing. Electron microscopes magnify cells about 2 MILLION times and provide incredible detail.

Good Save

French microbiologist and chemist Louis Pasteur (1822–1895) and Pierre Paul Émile Roux (1853–1933), a doctor and **bacteriologist**, worked together to develop a rabies vaccine for humans. In 1885, they administered the first rabies vaccine to nine-year-old Joseph Meister (1876–1940) after a rabid dog mauled him. During a period of 11 days, Pasteur gave Joseph 13 shots. The treatment proved a success, and Joseph didn't develop the deadly virus.

What's Different?

Study these images from two different types of microscopes. How are they different? How are they similar? Which one has more detail? Show them to a friend or classmate and see if they can tell which is which!

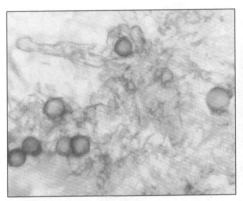

Pollen grains with a light microscope
Credit: Ergriffi (CC BY 4.0)

Pollen grains shown with an electron microscope

Yet, the patient feels miserable, wants relief, and demands medication. The doctor writes a prescription before lab results are in and the patient takes antibiotics they don't need and that don't help. This leads to overuse.

Sometimes, medication is misused. A patient might feel better after a few days on the medicine and doesn't finish all the pills, even though they are supposed to take them all. They might even save the remaining pills for the next time they don't feel well. Always follow your doctor's instructions when taking medication!

In the next chapter, we'll take a look at some bigger organisms and the impact they have on the world around us. Plants are everywhere, and without them, we couldn't survive! Let's find out why.

ESSENTIAL QUESTION

How do tiny organisms impact our lives?

NOW YOU DON'T SEE IT,
NOW YOU DO!

Spores are one-celled structures produced by fungi, which develop into new fungi. Mushrooms are umbrella-shaped fungi. You can make invisible mushroom spores visible!

> **Use any of these different types of mushrooms:** portobello, shiitake, white button (with dark gills), oyster, porcini, hedgehog, chanterelle, or morel. Flip a mushroom upside down. Pop off the stalk beneath the cap if there is one.

> **Investigate what's under the cap.** Does the mushroom have thin, papery gills that run under the cap toward the stem? Does it have lots of tiny holes, called **pores**? Or does it have long, thin "teeth" that hang down? These are all different structures mushrooms use to spread spores so more mushrooms can grow. If you have a mushroom with gills, run your fingertips over the gills. You should see a brownish powder come out. That powder contains microscopic spores.

24 H

BIO BOX
- some mushrooms
- paper
- glass bowl
- hairspray
- scrapbook or construction paper
- glue

WORDS TO KNOW

pore: a tiny opening through which substances pass.

> **At the center of a small sheet of paper or unlined index card,** position the mushroom with its underside down. Carefully place a glass bowl over it. Leave the mushroom on the paper for 24 hours.

> **After 24 hours, carefully lift the bowl.** Slip the mushroom off the paper. What do you see there?

> **Use hairspray to lock the spores in place.** Holding the sprayer about 12 inches above the paper, spray a thin layer over the print.

> **Use glue to mount your print on a sheet of scrapbook or construction paper.** Try this with all the mushrooms you have to compare the different prints they make.

Try This!

Mushrooms grow from spores, not seeds. Check out this video to discover how to plant and grow your own indoor mushroom farm.

🔎 YouTube how to grow mushrooms

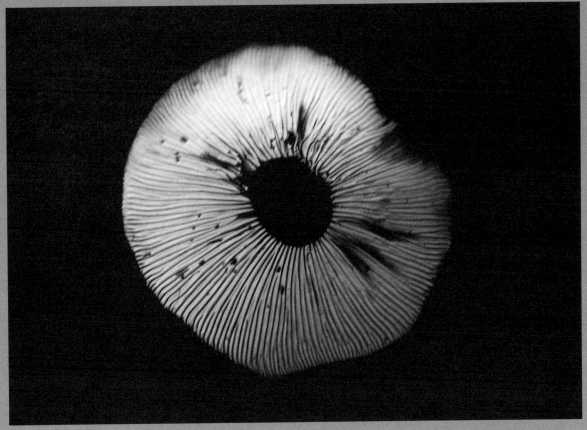

Credit: Ross Angus (CC BY 2.0)

COLLECT POND SAMPLES IN YOUR
OWN PLANKTON NET

BIO BOX
- old, light-colored pantyhose or tights
- thin wire
- small jar or bottle
- duct tape
- heavy thread or fishing line
- string
- key ring
- eye dropper
- slide
- microscope

Plankton form the first link in the **marine** food chain. Plankton are microscopic plants and animals that float at the surface of fresh and salt water. They provide food for other organisms. For example, in a tropical reef ecosystem, damselfish and fusiliers nibble plankton.

Make your own plankton net to collect samples. Will you discover "animalcules, a-swimming nimbly" when you view samples under a scope? Make a scientific method worksheet in your science journal to organize your experiment. Try to borrow a microscope if you don't have one.

> **Be Careful:** Wear a life jacket and always use caution around water. Ask an adult to help you collect samples. If you are boating on a lake, river, or ocean, slow way down and drag the net in the water behind you for a minute or two.

> **Cut one leg off the pantyhose or tights.**
To make the net, bend 20 inches of thin wire to form a circle. Secure the ends with duct tape. Roll the tights' "thigh" end over the wire circle. Use heavy thread or fishing line to sew it around the wire.

> **If there is one, cut the foot off the end.**
Slip the "ankle" end over the mouth of a small jar or bottle. Wind string or fishing line around the top of the jar. Tie it securely. Reinforce the tied area with duct tape.

> **Make the bridle to tow the net.** Cut four, 20-inch lengths of string. Securely tie them at four equal intervals around the circle. Draw the four loose ends through a key ring. Tie them tightly to form the bridle's ring.

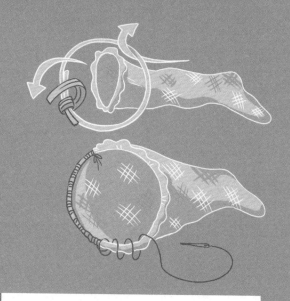

WORDS TO KNOW

plankton: microscopic plants and animals that float or drift in great numbers in bodies of water.

marine: having to do with the ocean.

Climate Change Corner

Millions of microscopic organisms with incredible biological diversity—algae, animals, bacteria, and viruses—live in the sunlit waters of ocean surfaces. They are essential to life on Earth. With warming oceans and changing ecosystems, how will plankton communities be impacted? How will not only marine food chains but also our own food chains change?

Explore these questions in this BBC Earth video.

🔎 BBC Earth plankton

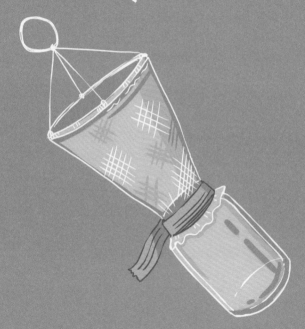

❯ **Cut a fifth length of string.** Tie it to the bridle ring so you can tow it for plankton samples. Find a safe location on a sturdy dock or pier. Wear a life jacket. Slowly walk up and down the dock towing the net through water to scoop samples into the bottle.

❯ **Back indoors, use an eye dropper to place drops of your water sample on a slide.** Examine the plankton under a microscope. Sketch the microorganisms you observe on your scientific method worksheet. Jot down descriptions. Conduct research to identify and label them.

Try This!

Plankton come in an amazing variety of colors, shapes, sizes, and textures. Visit the "Zoom Gallery" at Ask A Biologist. Use zoom tools to zero in on different types of plankton samples. How are samples alike? Different? Which samples do you find most intriguing?

🔎 Plankton Zoom Gallery

GROW MICROORGANISMS IN A
WINOGRADSKY COLUMN

You can't see microorganisms, but they are alive. Microorganisms need energy, water, and nutrients to thrive. Give them what they need! Build a Winogradsky column, an environment for microorganisms to grow. Use sunlight, newspaper, an egg yolk, and mucky soil to grow microbes in a bottle.

Caution: Ask an adult to help cut off the top of the bottle.

❯ **Choose a place where you can find mucky soil or sand.** A combination of mud and sand works well. You might select a freshwater pond or an ocean shore, your own garden, or a forest.

❯ **Wear garden gloves.** Use a small shovel or garden trowel to scoop out muck. Drop at least 5 cups into a small bucket. Pluck out rocks, twigs, shells, or leaves from the sample. Use a measuring cup to scoop about 5 cups of water from the same field site and drop it into another small bucket.

❯ **Back inside, remove the label from the 2-liter bottle.** Have an adult cut off the top third of the bottle to form a column. Set aside the top section to use as a funnel later.

❯ **Slowly add some water to the muck and mix with a paint stirrer as you pour.** Stir until the mixture reaches the consistency of thick cream. You don't want the mixture to be too watery, but make sure it remains fluid and moves freely. You'll need to pour it through the funnel later.

BIO BOX

- garden gloves
- trowel or small shovel
- 2 buckets
- measuring cup
- water
- clear, 2-liter bottle
- paint stirrer
- newspaper
- pencil sharpener
- chalk
- hard-boiled egg yolk
- plastic wrap
- rubber band
- duct tape

In one fistful of **SOIL**, you'll unearth hundreds or even thousands of different kinds of **MICROORGANISMS!**

❯ **Shred a piece of newspaper into tiny pieces and stir them into the mixture.** With a pencil sharpener, grind a piece of chalk. Measure 1 tablespoon of powdered chalk and stir it into the mixture. Place the hard-boiled egg yolk in a cup and crush it up with a fork. Add the yolk to the mixture.

❯ **Fit the funnel, neck end down, into the column's top.** Use duct tape to secure it in place. Scoop a small amount of mixture into the funnel. With one hand over the bottle's top, tap the bottle against the table. You're removing any oxygen inside and allowing the mixture to settle.

❯ **Repeat the process of adding small amounts of mixture and settling it at the bottom of the bottle.** Continue until the bottle is almost, but not completely, full.

❯ **Remove the funnel from the bottle.** Briskly stir the mixture to remove air bubbles. Allow the bottle to sit undisturbed. After half an hour, make sure water that has settled at the top of the bottle is about three-quarters of an inch deep. If necessary, pour out or add a bit of water.

❯ **Seal the top of the bottle with plastic wrap.** Use a rubber band to secure the wrap in place. Put the bottle in a bright location near a window but out of direct sunlight and away from heat. The bottle will stay in this location for four weeks.

Sergei Winogradsky (1856-1953) INVENTED the WINOGRADSKY COLUMN in the 1880s. It is still used for scientific study today!

❯ **Leave the bottle in place.** Try not to shift it when you come to study its progress during the four-week period. Make a scientific method worksheet to describe your experiment and record predictions of what changes will occur in the column through time.

❯ **For four weeks, check the column on the same day each week.** Create a colored sketch of your observations each time you study it. You will probably notice purplish and green blotches growing first. They appear at the side of the column facing sunlight. What other changes do you observe?

WHAT'S HAPPENING?

As time passes, microbes will grow in layers of different colors. They'll create their own ecosystem! Why are the microorganisms growing in layers? Oxygen concentration is highest at the top of the bottle. Microbes that need oxygen grow there, near the surface. Oxygen is lower at the bottom. Microorganisms that don't need much oxygen hang out there.

MICROORGANISMS AND
SEED SPEED

There's more to soil than meets the eye. The naked eye, that is. On your mark, get set, GO! Conduct a seed speed sprint to discover if seeds sprout when soil has no microorganisms in it.

❯ **Create a scientific method worksheet in your science journal to make predictions and record observations.** Then, go outside to locate fertile soil in your garden or a nature area. You'll know soil is fertile if plants are growing in it.

❯ **Wear garden gloves.** Carefully brush away leaf litter to reveal soil. Use a small shovel or garden trowel and old spoons to dig down about 2 inches. Place a soil sample on a paper plate. You'll want several large spoonfuls to later fill two jars halfway or more.

❯ **Lightly sift the sample.** Spread it out with your fingertips. Examine it with a magnifying glass. What do you see?

❯ **If you've unearthed critters such as roly-poly pill bugs and worms,** gently return them where you found them. Seal the rest of the sample in a plastic bag.

❯ **Indoors, preheat the oven to 180 degrees Fahrenheit.** Prepare two sticky notes, labeled "Uncooked Sample" and "Cooked Sample." Use two jars of equal size. Place one label on each jar.

❯ **Divide the soil into two equal parts.** Pour one into the "Uncooked Sample" jar for now. Set it aside. Pour the second into a pie pan.

Nature Detective

Dig it! Look below leaf litter and poke around at a shallow depth, at the ground level of the soil. This **topsoil** is composed of **silt**, sand, clay, and **organic** matter. Organic matter is decaying plants and animals. Depending on where you live and recent weather conditions, you might unearth water, too. You may discover rocks. Why is leaf litter thick in some places and thinner in others? Is soil different in these places, too? In your science journal, draw what your soil sample looks like. Can you identify different components? Do you find more organisms in soil under a thick layer of leaf litter or under a thinner layer? Why?

❯ **Place the pie pan in the oven for 20 minutes to kill any microorganisms.** With an adult's help, remove the sample from the oven and allow it to cool thoroughly.

❯ **While the soil cools, divide some bean seeds into two equal groups.** Plant one group in the "Uncooked Sample" jar. When the cooked sample cools, carefully place it in the "Cooked Sample" jar. Plant the second group of seeds in it.

❯ **Lightly water each jar of seeds.** Select a warm, sunny location for growth. For 10 days, provide the same amount of sunlight and water for each jar. Predict which sample will grow faster. Will microorganisms in soil help or hurt seeds?

Try This!

Watch this beautiful time-lapse film of a dwarf sunflower's life cycle! A seed sprouts, grows, and blooms into a full flower. In time, the flower wilts. How does the music add to the film's impact?

🔎 Life Cycle of a Sunflower Time Lapse

WORDS TO KNOW

topsoil: the top layer of soil.

silt: particles of fine soil, rich in nutrients.

organic: something that is or was living, such as animals, wood, grass, and insects.

43

Chapter 3

PLANTS
MAKE LIFE POSSIBLE

Look around your own environment. What plant life do you see? Here on Earth, plants are incredibly diverse. Patchy lichens are adapted for super-short Arctic growing seasons, while a prickly pear cactus resists withering in harsh deserts. Algae mostly exist in water, while towering redwood trees stretch tall toward the sky.

ESSENTIAL QUESTION

Why are plants essential to life on Earth?

No matter where you live, plants are all around you, not only outside, but maybe in your kitchen and on your windowsills! Let's take a closer look at these remarkable organisms living alongside us.

Imagine a meadow in late summer's sunshine. A weeping willow tree spreads out like an umbrella. It sways gently in the breeze. Sleek green leaves tickle clumps of yellow carpet moss at your feet. Fern fronds wave.

As you walk through the meadow, purple wildflowers peek over slender leaves. Bristly burrs crackle under your sneakers. Inside the burrs are sweet beechnut kernels, a favorite food of deer and wild turkeys. Blue jays squabble over juicy blackberries. Rabbits nibble tasty clover.

PLANTS ARE LIVING THINGS

Plants in the meadow, like plants everywhere on Earth, make life possible. All animals depend on plants for survival. They provide the food we eat and the oxygen we breathe. Without plants, Earth's **atmosphere** couldn't support life.

Scientists estimate there are at least 390,900 known species of plants on Earth. Botanists discover and describe about 2,000 new plant species annually. Sadly, many are in danger of **extinction**. Scientists estimate extinction threatens 21 percent of all plant species. Plant extinction is caused by pests and disease, **habitat** loss, **invasive species**, and climate change.

Sometimes, it's easy to forget that plants are living things. Maybe that's because we don't see them moving in front of us the way we see animals constantly in motion. But what about that glorious moment when flower buds burst open to welcome spring? What about the nutritious vegetables grown from plants you've nurtured in your garden?

Plants are moving, but their movement is so slow we can't watch it happen. Plants run their own food factories. In fact, thousands of **chemical reactions** and processes take place inside plant cells every second!

> **WORDS TO KNOW**
>
> **lichen:** a plant-like organism made of algae and fungus that grows on solid surfaces such as rocks or trees.
>
> **atmosphere:** the mixture of gases surrounding a planet.
>
> **extinction:** the disappearance of a species from the world.
>
> **habitat:** the natural area where a plant or animal lives.
>
> **invasive species:** a species that is not native to an ecosystem and that rapidly expands to crowd out other species.
>
> **chemical reaction:** the change of a substance into a new substance.

PLANTS were the first **ORGANISMS** adapted to life on **LAND**. It's on land that plants can capture more intense **SUNLIGHT** to perform food-making wonders.

WORDS TO KNOW

seed: the part of a plant that holds all the beginnings of a plant.

root: the underground plant structure that anchors the plant and takes in water and minerals from soil.

stem: the plant structure that supports leaves, flowers, and fruits.

pollen: a fine, yellow powder produced by flowering plants. Pollen fertilizes the seeds of other plants as it gets spread around by the wind, birds, and insects.

photosynthesis: the process by which plants produce food, using light as energy.

stomata: tiny pores on the outside of leaves that allow gases and water vapor to pass in and out.

carbon dioxide: a gas formed by the burning of fossil fuels, the rotting of plants and animals, and the breathing out of animals, including humans.

water vapor: the gas form of water.

aquatic: living or growing in water.

arthritis: a medical condition that causes swollen joints, stiffness, and pain.

PLANT STRUCTURE

Plants grow from **seeds** and have **roots**, **stems**, and leaves. Most plants also produce flowers and fruits. Each of these plant parts tackles a special job.

Flowers are the showy part of a plant. They play an important role in the reproductive process—their colors and smells attract insects and birds that spread **pollen**. A plant's fruits can be sweet and tasty, but they also protect seeds. And seeds create new plants. Inside a seed are the energy and materials a plant needs for growth until it sprouts its first leaves above the ground.

Roots, stems, and leaves are not reproductive parts. Sprawling underground, hairy roots are anchors that hold plants in place. Roots suck water and minerals from soil. They also store any extra food.

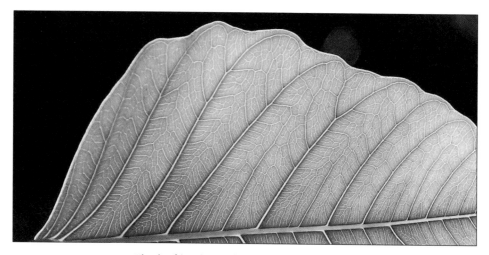

The leaf is where photosynthesis happens!

Sturdy stems prop up plants and provide support for leaves, flowers, and fruits. Stems also transport water and food to a plant's roots and leaves.

Leaves are in charge of producing food for the whole plant. In fact, leaves are the core part of the food factories where sunlight gets turned into food through **photosynthesis**. **Stomata** dot the outside of leaves. Like mini mouths, these pores open and shut, allowing **carbon dioxide** gas to enter the plant and **water vapor** and oxygen to exit the plant. Most land plants contain stomata on the bottom of their leaves and most **aquatic** plants contain them on the top.

People have used
PLANTS IN MEDICINES
since ancient times.
Ancient Egyptians and Greeks chewed WILLOW BARK to ease headaches and arthritis pain.
Present-day scientists discovered willow bark contains SALICIN. This is very similar to the
ACETYLSALICYLIC ACID
used in the modern painkiller, aspirin!

WORDS TO KNOW

convert: to change.

evolve: to change or develop gradually.

carbohydrate: the sugar that is the source of food and energy in a plant.

translocation: movement of water, sugar, and minerals through a plant.

xylem: the tubes in plants through which nutrients travel.

phloem: the structures within plants that bring sugar made during photosynthesis to different parts of the plant.

glucose: the simple sugar that plants produce through photosynthesis.

Scientists theorize that **PHOTOSYNTHESIS** evolved more than **3 BILLION YEARS** ago, not long after the first organism appeared on Earth. Scientists think that before that time, Earth's atmosphere didn't contain **OXYGEN.**

TOGETHER WITH LIGHT

Photosynthesis is the process green plants and some algae use to produce food. The word *photo* means "light." *Synthesis* means "putting together." Photosynthesis means "putting together with light." So, it's not surprising that this amazing process requires sunlight. Plants **convert** light from the sun into the energy they need to grow.

In addition to sunlight, what other ingredients do plants use to make food? Water (H_2O) from soil and carbon dioxide (CO_2) from air. Above and below ground, plant parts put these ingredients to work.

Photosynthesis mainly takes place in leaves, where chloroplasts filled with green chlorophyll collect the sun's energy and put it to use. Chloroplasts turn sunlight, H_2O, and CO_2 into **carbohydrates**, or simple sugars, that are the plant's food.

Plants for Lunch

What's the difference between a fruit and a vegetable? A vegetable is a part of a plant that's eaten, such as leaves (spinach), stems (celery), roots (carrots), and flowers (cauliflower). To botanists, a fruit is the ripened part of a plant that develops from the female reproductive part. Fruit is located at the base of a flower. It contains the plant's seed or seeds. Inside fruits, you'll find seeds from flowering plants. So, what are tomatoes, avocados, and olives? Fruits or veggies? They're fruits people typically eat as veggies!

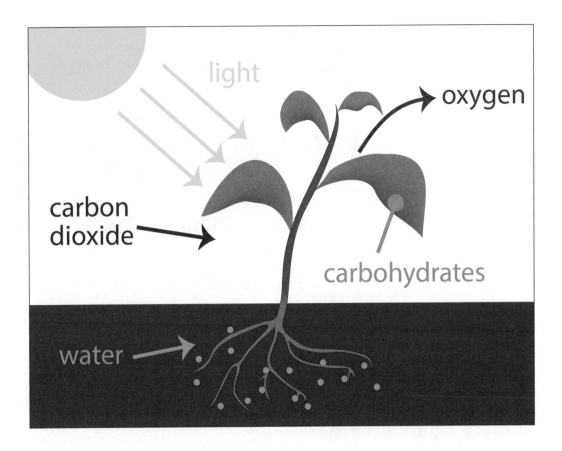

Water, sugar, and minerals move through plants in a process called **translocation**. A tissue called **xylem** carries water and minerals from roots to stems and leaves. **Phloem**, another tissue, moves sugary food made during photosynthesis to parts of the plant that don't make food, such as roots, where the food is stored as a simple sugar called **glucose**.

AIR PURIFIERS

Plants keep our air clean! They produce clean oxygen, a gas necessary for animals and people to survive. Plants don't breathe the way we do, but they do take air in and let it out. Animals and people breathe in oxygen and breathe out carbon dioxide. Plants do the reverse.

BACKYARD BIOLOGY

A stomata on the leaf of a tomato plant

Through stomata, plants take in carbon dioxide. As they breathe in, they also remove **toxins** and **pollutants** from the air. Clean oxygen exits the stomata as a waste product. At the same time, in a process called **transpiration**, stomata release water vapor. About 10 percent of moisture found in the atmosphere comes from plants.

Climate Change Corner

The largest forest in the world, Brazil's Amazon rainforest is nicknamed "the lungs of the planet." The Amazon's abundant plant life purifies our air. It cleans air of carbon dioxide, a major greenhouse gas. Through photosynthesis, plants use energy from sunlight, water from soil, and carbon dioxide from air to make food. Plants release oxygen, which people and animals require for life.

The Amazon is in flames. The human-made emergency threatens our world's climate. In 2019, the Amazon experienced a record number of forest fires. Around 76,000 fires raged, an astonishing increase of 84% over 2018. With Brazil's weakened environmental protections, the Amazon lost nearly 7,200 square miles of precious forest cover. That's about the size of New Jersey!

During the G7 summit in August 2019, world leaders sounded the alarm. They united to combat this environmental emergency. They pledged $20 million dollars to fight the blazing fires.

Feed Me!

Some plants evolved as meat-eaters that snare and devour insects. Venus flytraps look like they're from, well, Venus. In the wild, they grow in North and South Carolina's **bogs**. The soil there does not have the minerals the plants need, so Venus flytraps rely instead on specialized leaves that take in nutrients as the plant feasts on flesh. Here's how! Each flytrap looks like a clam with bristly teeth. Lined with trigger hairs, the flytrap leaves hang open like a gaping mouth. Sweet nectar lures flies, spiders, bees, and moths inside. When the prey brushes against the leaves' trigger hairs—snap! The flytrap clamps shut. The trapdoor stays closed while the plant slowly digests dinner, which can take two weeks! Then, the trapdoor springs open to welcome the next victim.

Learn about another carnivorous plant, the pitcher plant!

🔎 BBC carnivorous plants

BEEF-AND-BEAN BURRITO BREAKDOWN

Plants don't feed only themselves. As producers in food chains and food webs, they provide nourishment for animals and people, too.

People get most of their nutrition from plants. Sometimes, you go straight to the source. You snack on a crunchy apple or munch baby carrots. Other times, it's more complicated. Consider the beef-and-bean burrito you might be having for lunch.

Plants **FLOURISH** in every **ENVIRONMENT** on the planet. They are **ADAPTED TO SURVIVE** in the extreme ecosystems of broiling **DESERTS** and frigid **ARCTIC REGIONS**.

symbiosis: a relationship between two different species of organisms in which each benefits from the other.

The ingredients in your burrito are beef, beans, salsa, and tortillas. Beef comes from cows, which graze on grasses. Beans are seeds from bean plants. Diced tomatoes and onions make up salsa—tomatoes grow on vines and onions are edible bulbs that grow underground.

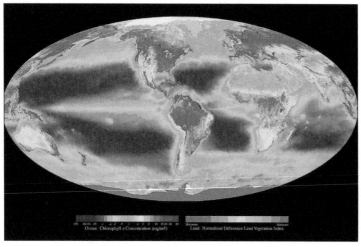

This map shows where the most photosynthesis is happening on both land and sea—the darker areas are where the most oxygen is being produced by plants.

But what about the tortillas? How are they made from plants? Flour for tortillas is ground from cereal grains, which are small seeds or fruits. Even the dab of guacamole and a sprinkle of olives you may have on the side come from plants. Guacamole is made from mashed avocado, which grows on trees. And olives grow on . . . olive trees.

You can now see how plants are essential to life on our planet. So, how to make sure they're always around? Let's find out more about the life cycle of plants.

ESSENTIAL QUESTION

Why are plants essential to life on Earth?

Symbiosis

Lichens are made up of algae and fungi growing in **symbiosis**. This is a relationship between two organisms that rely on each other. It's a win-win partnership that's beneficial for both. How do the algae and fungi in lichens help each other? Algae contain chlorophyll and produce food from the sun's energy. Fungi protect the algae. In return, fungi gain nutrients from the algae.

FLOWER-POUNDING
T-SHIRT

BIO BOX
- fresh flowers, such as geraniums, hollyhocks, impatiens, pansies, phlox, zinnias
- garden gloves
- scissors or pruners
- plastic containers with lids
- collection bag
- wax paper
- tweezers
- white T-shirt
- rubber mallet
- clean rags
- fabric marker
- table salt
- water
- plastic tub

Harvest vibrant flowers at peak bloom and pound petals to create a printed image on a T-shirt. If you can, use a T-shirt labeled "PFD." That means it's prepared for dying so it will hold the flower colors.

Caution: Ask an adult for help when you use scissors.

❯ **Head out to pick and snip flowers.** Choose flowers at peak bloom, when they are rich with color. Flowers that have begun to wilt won't work as well. Wear garden gloves, and with an adult's help, snip flowers from the top of the stem. Seal flowers in plastic containers and put the containers in the collection bag.

❯ **Spread wax paper over a table or other sturdy surface.** Place your flowers on the paper. Snip away any remaining bits of stem. With tweezers, remove everything from inside the flower so you have just petals. Arrange the petals to create a design you like.

❯ **Carefully place the shirt's front on top of the flower-covered wax paper.** Use a rubber mallet to gently pound the shirt over each area of flowers. To prevent smearing, wipe the mallet on a clean rag each time you pound flowers of different colors.

❯ **Lift the shirt away from the wax paper.** Place it face-up on the table to dry thoroughly. Then, use the fabric marker to carefully outline each flower print.

Try This!

Chile's Atacama Desert is one of the planet's driest regions. In August 2017, torrential rains pelted the desert. Almost overnight, a super bloom erupted. Thousands of flowers covered the region. Read this *National Geographic* article and watch the video to explore the *desierto florido* (flowering desert). Why did flowers sprout?

🔎 Atacama Desert flower boom

❯ **Combine ½ cup table salt and 8 cups water in the plastic tub.** Place the shirt in the tub to soak for about 30 minutes. Then, hang the shirt up to dry. You'll find that the flower images will fade over time. How can you preserve them? Try turning the shirt inside out when it's time to wash it. Then, hand wash and hang to dry.

PLANT PARTS SALAD

Toss a colorful, nutritious plant salad! Harvest ingredients from your home garden if you have one or check out a farmer's market or grocery store to round up produce. Challenge yourself to try something new and exciting. How about fresh fennel or jicama? Star fruit or zucchini blossoms?

> **Caution:** Ask an adult to help with any chopping and with any ingredients that require cooking. Make sure all ingredients come from a safe source. Don't eat anything picked from public places because they may have been sprayed with **pesticides**.

> **Select ingredients.** Choose one ingredient from each of the following categories: leaves, flowers, stems, fruits, roots, seeds, and nuts.

* leaves: cabbage, kale, lettuce, spinach, turnip greens

* flowers: broccoli, cauliflower, nasturtium, squash blossoms, zucchini blossoms

* stems: asparagus, bamboo shoot, celery, fennel, Swiss chard

* fruits: apple, avocado, orange, star fruit, tomato

* roots: beet, carrot, jicama, onion, shallot

* seeds: black-eyed peas, edamame, garbanzo beans, pinto beans, or ¼ cup seeds such as sunflower seeds

* nuts: slivered almonds, hazelnuts, halved pecans, pine nuts, chopped walnuts

> **Wash your hands.** Then, wash the fresh fruits and vegetables. Allow them to drain or dry gently with a clean towel. If you're using frozen or canned ingredients, prepare them according to the directions. You might need to strain some of the food.

Across the planet, **SOIL** holds a whopping **2,500 gigatons** of **CARBON**! Each year, soil removes and captures approximately **25 percent** of the planet's **FOSSIL FUEL** emissions.

WORDS TO KNOW

pesticide: a chemical used to kill pests such as insects.

carbon: an element that is found in all life on Earth and in coal, petroleum, and diamonds.

emission: something sent or given off, such as smoke, gas, heat, or light.

> **Leaves form the bulk of the salad!** Ask an adult to help you use a knife to chop, shred, or cut leaves into bite-sized pieces. Place the greens into a large bowl.

> **Slice flowers and cut stems for variety and nutrition.** Add them to the bowl.

> **Fruits add special zing!** Peel fruit as necessary. Remove any pits or seeds. Cut into pieces and add them to the bowl.

> **Time for protein with crunchy texture!** Add seeds to the mix (¼ to ½ cup is probably enough). Add about ¼ cup nuts.

> **Toss the salad gently using spoons or tongs to mix all the ingredients.** Serve with your favorite dressing.

Try This!

Is your school or family part of the Meatless Monday movement? More than 40 countries across the globe united to lower meat consumption and eat a more plant-based diet.

Visit the Meatless Monday website. Read the introductory info and watch the video to explore the movement's 100-year history and the ways people today band together to help our planet. Then, conduct additional research. Learn how eating less meat helps the environment.

🔎 Meatless Monday

Watch this video about the relationship between soil, food, and the climate. What steps can we take to make sure soil stays healthy?

🔎 Michael Pollan soil

COOL
COLORS

What color pops to mind when you think of a leaf? Green, right? But is green the only pigment present? Create leaf rubbings and treat them to reveal their true colors!

> **Caution:** Ask an adult for help. Use caution with rubbing alcohol. Work in an area that's well **ventilated**. Alcohol is **flammable**. Do not splash it into your eyes or onto your skin and dispose of it properly after you finish the activity.

> **Create a scientific method worksheet** in your science journal to record predictions and observations. Wear a lab coat or long-sleeved shirt and goggles.

> **Cut a coffee filter into three strips** approximately 1 inch wide and 4 inches long so they fit inside the jar and are long enough to stick out the top. The length of the strips will depend on the height of your jar.

> **Use one large leaf from each of the three different plants.** Turn the leaf from the first plant upside down. Place it on one filter strip, about 1 inch from the bottom. With a pencil point, rub gently on the leaf. Create a rubbing on the strip about the size of a penny. Reposition the leaf. Continue rubbing the same area to darken the spot on the filter. Repeat with the other two leaves, using a fresh filter strip for each.

> **Ask an adult to fill the jar with ½ inch of rubbing alcohol.** Tape the filter strips vertically around the jar's inside. The bottom of the strips should touch the bottom of the jar.

> **After some time, the alcohol should travel to the top of the strips.** Once the alcohol has reached the top, put on gloves and remove the strips with tweezers. Allow the strips to dry on newspaper. Study the strips. What pigments did you reveal?

WHAT'S HAPPENING?

You might notice shades of brown, red, orange, and yellow—fall colors in many areas of North America. Those pigments are always present in leaves. Why can't you always see them? Chlorophyll's lush green shades of spring and summer conceal the others.

BIO BOX

- science journal and pencil
- lab coat or long-sleeved shirt
- safety goggles
- coffee filter
- small, clear glass jar
- large leaves from 3 different plants
- pencil
- rubbing alcohol
- protective gloves, such as vinyl or rubber
- tweezers
- newspaper

WORDS TO KNOW

ventilate: to supply fresh air into a room or enclosed place.

flammable: something that burns very easily.

Chapter 4

PLANT
LIFE CYCLES

Food and fruits. Fibers and fuel. Fields of flowers. These are all ways that plants enrich our lives. As we saw in the last chapter, plants are essential to our survival. If we run out of plants, we're all in trouble. Plants have adapted to life on Earth by adopting ways to keep their species thriving—how do they do it?

Do you have any flowers outside where you live? What kinds? Flowers have very important jobs, besides looking pretty. A flower has one main function—to produce seeds. Most seeds start out tiny. In the right conditions, they flourish and grow to produce new plants. Let's find out how they do this.

ESSENTIAL QUESTION

How do plants reproduce?

WORDS TO KNOW

pistil: the female, seed-producing reproductive part of a flower. It includes the ovary, style, and stigma.

stigma: the upper part of the pistil, which receives pollen.

style: the stalk-like tube that extends from the ovary in a flower to support the stigma.

ovary: the part of the pistil in a flower that bears ovules and ripens into a fruit.

ovule: a small structure that develops into a seed after it joins with a grain of pollen.

stamen: the male, pollen-producing reproductive part of a flower. It includes the filament and anther.

filament: the stalk that supports the anther in a flower.

anther: the flower part that produces and holds pollen.

fertilize: to join female and male cells to produce seeds and offspring.

dissect: to cut something apart to study what's inside.

anatomy: the internal structure of an organism.

petals: the showy, brightly colored outer area of a flower.

MALES AND FEMALES?

Flowers can have all male parts or all female parts, but many have a combination of both. The male and female parts make seeds. How? An egg cell from the female part and a germ cell from a grain of pollen in the male part join to become seeds.

The **pistil** is the female, seed-producing organ, usually located right in the middle of the flower. If you touch the top of the pistil, you'll notice a sticky opening. That's the **stigma**. During reproduction, the stigma grabs male pollen grains.

The **style** is a tube shaped like a stalk. The style supports the stigma. At the bottom of the style is a bulgy, pear-shaped **ovary**. The ovary holds eggs, or **ovules**.

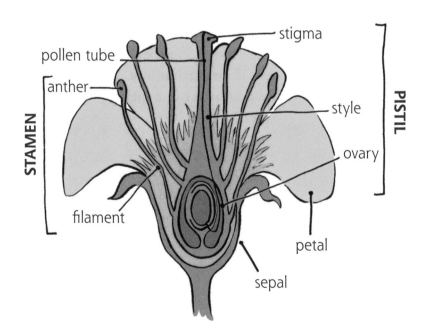

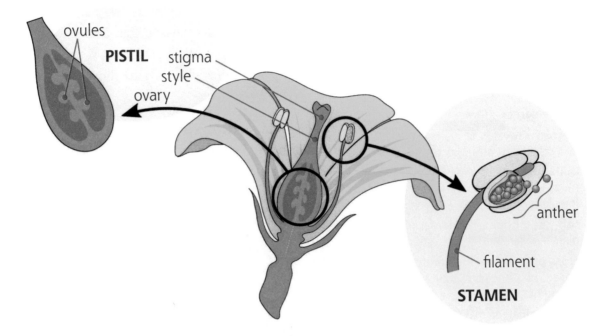

The **stamen** is a flower's male, pollen-producing organ. Not all flowers contain the same number of stamens, but all stamens have two parts, the **filament** and the **anther**. The filament is a thread-like stalk that holds up the anther. The anther produces pollen, which is often yellow. This sticky, dusty powder contains male reproductive cells, called germ cells. When the germ cell of a pollen grain joins an egg cell, the egg is **fertilized**. Then, the ovary ripens into a fruit and the ovules become seeds.

Look Inside

You can **dissect** a flower to investigate its **anatomy**. Check first to make sure a bee or other pollinator isn't inside or buzzing around! Pick a flower at peak bloom. Daffodils, gladiolus, lilies, and tulips make great specimens. With your fingers, gently pluck away **petals** one by one. How are they designed to attract pollinators? Remove other parts. Can you identify the pistil and stamen and their components? Rub pollen between your fingertips. What's the texture? Draw your observations in your science journal.

WORDS TO KNOW

sepals: the special leaves that enclose a flower.

pollinator: an insect or other animal that transfers pollen from the male part of a flower to the female part of a flower.

nectar: a sweet fluid made by flowers that attracts insects.

pollination: the process of transferring male pollen to the female stigma.

self-pollination: the transfer of a plant's pollen onto its own stigma.

cross-pollination: the transfer of pollen from one plant to the stigma of another plant.

mammal: an animal such as a human, dog, or cat. Mammals are born live, feed milk to their young, and usually have hair or fur.

Flowering plants also contain **sepals**. These protective leaves are tucked under outer leaves and petals. Sepals keep young buds safe until they are ready to show their beautiful flowers.

Magenta, apricot, lavender! Have you ever wondered why petals come in such a dazzling range of colors and an abundance of shapes? It's because plants are fixed in place, so they have to put on a show to attract **pollinators**.

Showy, sweet-scented flowers welcome pollinators with promises of yummy **nectar**. Cushy petals are pillows for bees and wasps that hang out to enjoy a leisurely meal.

A hibiscus flower with yellow stamens and red pistils
Credit: Ray in Manila (CC BY 2.0)

WELCOME, POLLINATORS!

Plant reproduction depends on **pollination**—the transfer of pollen to the stigma. Sometimes one plant's pollen falls directly onto its own stigma. This process is called **self-pollination**. But how does **cross-pollination** happen between plants on opposite ends of a meadow?

Do you have ALLERGIES? Many people are allergic to POLLEN. Some plants produce lots and lots of pollen and scatter that pollen into the winds instead of relying on POLLINATORS. Achoo!

Wind and rain scatter pollen. Bees, butterflies, and birds also do the trick. Even small **mammals**, including scurrying mice and swooping bats, spread a plant's reproductive cells.

Imagine a yellow jacket as it bobs and weaves through a field of flowers and hovers over the blooms. The insect perches on a flower's soft petals and sips nectar, a plant's sugary liquid. When it crawls inside to get nectar from the pistil, the powdery pollen clings to the yellow jacket's fuzzy hind legs. As the yellow jacket buzzes off to drink another flower's nectar, pollen from the first flower settles onto the stigma of the next to fertilize ovules.

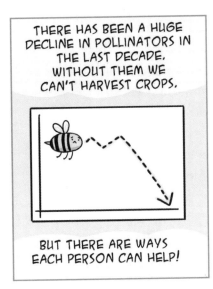

THERE HAS BEEN A HUGE DECLINE IN POLLINATORS IN THE LAST DECADE. WITHOUT THEM WE CAN'T HARVEST CROPS.

BUT THERE ARE WAYS EACH PERSON CAN HELP!

DESIGNATING EVEN A SMALL PART OF YOUR YARD TO BE A NATIVE FLOWER GARDEN REALLY HELPS POLLINATORS.

IT'S ALSO IMPORTANT NOT TO USE PESTICIDES.

LOOK UP WHAT PLANTS AND FLOWERS ARE NATIVE IN YOUR AREA AND HELP THE ENVIRONMENT!

WORDS TO KNOW

seed coat: the hard, protective covering on a seed.

embryo: a tiny plant inside a seed.

radicle: the first part of a plant embryo that emerges and forms a root.

plumule: the part of a plant embryo that forms a shoot.

germinate: to sprout and begin to grow.

cotyledon: the first leaves produced by a seed.

PACKED FOR THE TRIP OF A LIFETIME

A plant seed is a suitcase of life packed by the parent plant. On the outside, the **seed coat** keeps the seed from getting dried out or waterlogged. Inside is everything a new plant needs to spread roots, grow strong, and develop into an adult.

The **embryo** is the baby plant, in its earliest stages of development. Inside are the **radicle** and **plumule**. As the seed **germinates**, the radicle pops out. It becomes the baby plant's first root. Other roots branch out and develop as the plant grows and changes. The plumule provides the baby plant's first shoot. In time, the shoot becomes a stem and leaves.

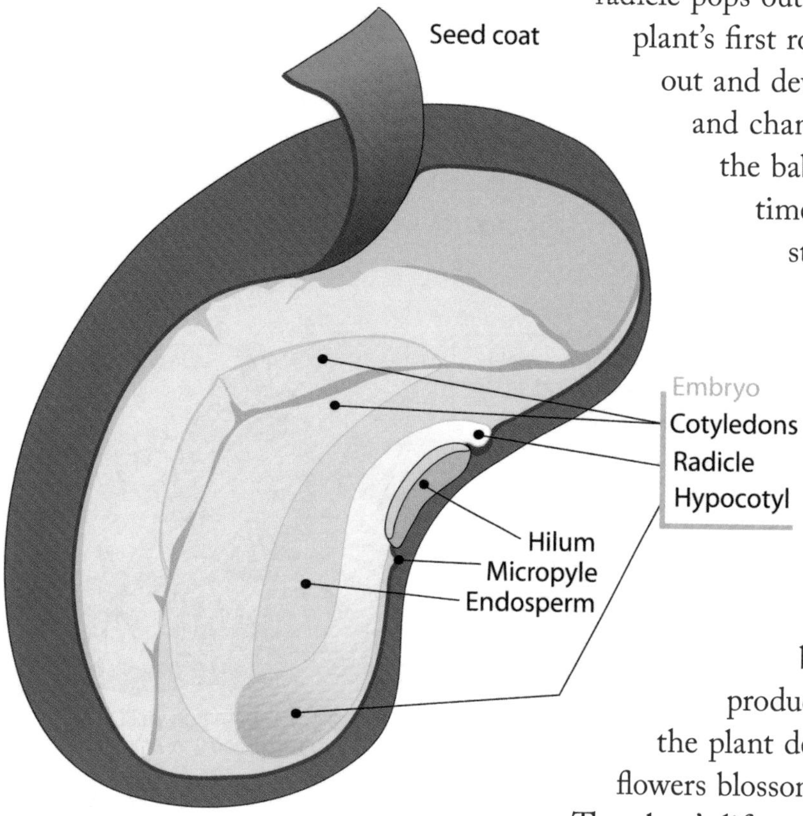

Cotyledons are the first leaves the plant produces. Their food storage tissues contain a stash of food that the young plant uses until it has enough leaves to begin photosynthesis and produce its own meals. When the plant develops into an adult, flowers blossom to attract pollinators. The plant's life cycle rolls on and on!

Seed coat

Embryo
Cotyledons
Radicle
Hypocotyl

Hilum
Micropyle
Endosperm

North America's **MONARCH BUTTERFLIES** are in trouble. Their population has dwindled by **90 PERCENT!** In 1998, more than **1 BILLION** monarch butterflies in the United States took to the skies and migrated south of the border to Mexico. By 2014, that number shriveled to **60 MILLION.** What caused this devastating decline of **PRECIOUS POLLINATORS?** Habitat loss in both countries.

Climate Change Corner

With Earth's consistently warming temperatures, some ecosystems experience shorter winters and earlier snow melt—spring arrives too soon. This means the critical timing of flowering and pollination gets thrown out of whack and plant-pollinator relationships can tumble out of sync. Plants bloom too early, weeks or even months ahead of schedule, and there are no pollinators yet to help with fertilization. Butterflies emerge from cocoons too late—plants have already died off and can't provide the nectar that serves as the butterflies' food. Bees buzz around too late and there's no pollen to feast on. Pollinators die and plant reproduction fails, weakening the ecosystem. This is another reason why it's important for everyone to join together to find solutions to the problem of climate change.

Read this blog post from Amy E. Boyd, ecologist and professor of biology. How do Boyd's experiences reflect the impact of climate change?

🔎 UCSUSA pollinators climate

tropism: a plant's involuntary response to a change in its environment.

stimulus: a change in an organism's environment that causes an action, activity, or response.

constrict: to become smaller.

gravity: a force that pulls all objects to Earth.

geotropism: plant growth in response to the force of gravity, which makes the roots grow downwards.

phototropism: plant growth in response to light, which makes the leaves grow or bend toward a light source.

auxin: a chemical in a plant that causes leaves to bend and lengthen.

hormone: a chemical in a plant that controls functions such as plant growth and fruit ripening.

thigmotropism: the response of a plant to physical contact.

TROPISM

Indoors, you might have observed a houseplant's stem and leaves bent toward sunlight streaming from a window. Outdoors, you've probably seen twisty vines coiled around a garden stake, chain fence, or tree. Unlike animals, plants have no legs and can't take a walk. But that doesn't mean they can't move! It only seems that way!

A plant's growth is affected by **tropism**, an automatic response to a **stimulus**. Stimulus and response are similar to cause and effect. For example, when you go outside into bright sunlight, the pupils of your eyes **constrict** and become smaller. The stimulus, which is light, causes the response—dilation. You don't control the response. It happens on its own, automatically.

Gravity, light, and water cause plant growth. Have you wondered why a plant's roots grow downward? It's the result of **geotropism**. The force of gravity pulls roots down into soil. **Phototropism** causes a plant to grow toward a light source.

Nature Hunt

Hunt for evidence of phototropism in a forest preserve or wooded area. You might observe plants sprouting on the forest floor. Are they lengthening to reach a better environmental condition for growth? Can you find seedlings sprouting in shade from larger plants? What twists and turns do seedlings make to reach toward sunlight?

Phototropism at work in lentil sprouts

Credit: Russell Neches (CC BY 2.0)

Auxin, a plant **hormone**, causes leaves to bend and get longer. Leaves lengthen and stretch to snatch more rays. Auxin in a climbing plant's tendril makes shoots longer and stronger. Through **thigmotropism**, a plant may respond to something it touches. This is why a tendril coils around a branch when it feels it or it loops around a trellis, flowerpot, or other surface.

This movement is part of how plants survive, even without arms and legs. Next time you take a walk outside, look around and spot plants on the move!

Many wildflowers **SPROUT** in protected areas. You might not be aware of which areas are **PROTECTED**. Before you uproot any wildflowers and plants, remember to find out if you are in a protected area and get **PERMISSION** first.

ESSENTIAL QUESTION

How do plants reproduce?

65

HEY,
GEOTROPISM!

Sprout bean plants inside a clear cup. What will happen as gravitational pull works its wonders?

❯ **Crumple a paper towel so it fits inside the cup.** Pour water over the towel so it's thoroughly wet but not drenched.

❯ **Press three pinto beans between the towel and the side of the cup.** This makes a window for you to peek through as the beans sprout! Arrange seeds in three different positions—for example, tilted, vertical, and horizontal.

❯ **Start a scientific method worksheet in your science journal.** Write a hypothesis about how your different seeds will grow. How will gravity impact root growth? In which direction or directions will roots grow?

Watch this astonishing time-lapse video of phototropism and thigmatrophism in action!

🔍 phototropism geotropism time lapse

> **Check your seeds for growth every day for two weeks and then assess your hypothesis.** Add water when necessary to keep the paper towel wet.

Try This!

Repeat the activity, this time using quick-sprouting seeds instead of beans. You might use radish, watermelon, or marigold seeds. How do your results compare?

How Plants Use Thigmotropism

As tendrils grow around poles, walls, or anything else they come in contact with, their roots are doing the opposite! Plant roots practice negative thigmotropism. That means they avoid anything they come in contact with as they extend through the soil. This makes it easier for them to take the path of least resistance. What does this mean for geotropism? The roots will still grow downward as they try to avoid obstacles such as rocks, other roots, and anything else buried in the soil.

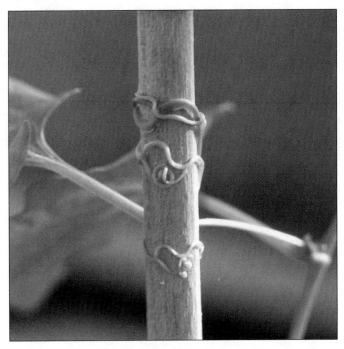

Tendrils are specialized stems that extend from the plant. They grasp the stake for support.

Credit: U.S. Department of Agriculture, Agricultural Research Service

YOU ARE MY
SUNSHINE

BIO BOX
° science journal and pencil
° large outdoor plant
° tape measure
° twist ties
° small brown paper bag
° colored cellophane

Investigate photosynthesis! Compare the growth of a plant's leaves when they receive different amounts of sunlight. How does each respond to light? Select a plant large enough to isolate three sections of leaves. If you can't find one, then try using three different plants of the same species. You'll observe leaves for almost a week, so choose a site where your project can remain undisturbed.

❭ **Start a scientific method worksheet in your science journal.** Draw a three-column chart. Label the columns: "Direct Sunlight," "Indirect Sunlight," "No Sunlight."

❭ **Select a large outdoor plant in your backyard or somewhere else where you have permission to do this activity.** Measure three sections of clustered leaves roughly the same size. For example, if you use a garden tomato plant, then you might measure three different 5-inch leaf clusters.

❭ **Choose one leaf cluster to represent each column of your chart.** In the appropriate column, note the length and width of the cluster's individual leaves. Count and write down the number of healthy leaves. Draw an illustration of each section of leaves.

❭ **Lightly wind a twist tie around your Direct Sunlight cluster,** right at the point where leaves connect with the stem. Make sure the tie isn't too tight.

❭ **Place a small brown bag over the No Sunlight cluster.** Secure the bag's open end with a second twist tie.

5"

❯ **Wrap colored cellophane around the Indirect Sunlight cluster.** Secure it with a third twist tie.

❯ **Predict what will happen to each section of leaves during a five-day period.** Which do you think will show the most growth? The greatest health? Why?

❯ **Observe and measure the leaves every day.** Take notes and make sketches in your journal. Have leaf sizes changed? Has the number of healthy leaves changed? Make an illustration of the leaves each time you check them. What conclusions do you draw about the amount of sunlight plants require to photosynthesize?

Try This!

Researchers at Arizona State University study ways to speed the process of photosynthesis. With a friend or family member, read this article. Why do researchers believe photosynthesis can aid world hunger?

🔎 ASU lab studies photosynthesis

A-MAZING! PHOTOTROPISM
IN A SHOEBOX

Sometimes, we forget plants are living things because they're fixed in place. Build a maze inside a shoebox and observe what happens when a bean plant tries to grow toward a light source.

▶ **Fill a small pot or cup with potting soil.** Plant three bean seeds. Lightly water the soil and place your container in a sunny location for one week. Keep the soil moist.

▶ **While you're waiting for the beans to sprout, prepare the maze.** Paint the inside of a shoebox black. Allow the paint to dry completely. Draw a circle at one end of the box and cut it out.

▶ **Cut out three panels from the cardboard approximately half the size of the box width.** Stand the box vertically with the end containing the circle facing up. Place the plant temporarily inside the box, at the bottom, to make sure you allow enough room for it. Arrange cardboard panels inside the box to form a maze. Remove the plant. Tape the panels securely in place.

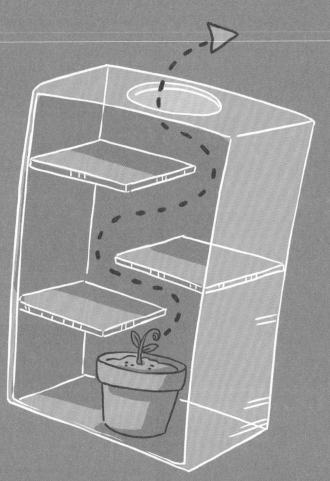

70

Sometimes, plants grow away from objects, as they do in this example of what's called crown shyness.
Credit: Dag Peak (CC BY 2.0)

❯ **After the beans sprout, stand the maze vertically, circle up.** Place the plant in position at the bottom of the maze. Secure the cover on the box.

❯ **Place the box on a window ledge or in a direct source of sunlight for two weeks.** Start a scientific method worksheet in your science journal. Open the lid every day to check on the plant and write your observations in your journal. Keep the soil moist but not drenched.

❯ **What a-mazing plant responses do you observe?** Is your bean plant growing? In what direction? In your science journal, describe the way your plant is growing.

Try This!

Sprout a second bean plant as a control. Place the second plant next to the maze, in the same light source. Compare and contrast the results after two weeks.

71

EGG-CENTRIC
EGGHEADS

Sprout different seeds in eggshells decorated with kooky faces. Then, compare results!

Caution: Handling raw eggs can cause illness, so wash your hands thoroughly after handling.

❯ **Decorate two 6-inch strips of card stock with colored permanent markers.** Then make two stands by forming each strip into a ring. Secure the rings with glue. Hold them in place as the glue sets.

❯ **Ask an adult to help you remove the tops of two raw eggs,** pour out the contents, and wash the shells gently in soapy water.

❯ **After the eggshells are dry,** carefully use markers and glue odds and ends to decorate them just for fun. Decorations might include googly eyes, broken jewelry, beads, fabric, or ribbon remnants.

❯ **Use a spoon to carefully fill each eggshell with ½ cup potting soil.** Sprinkle 1 teaspoon grass seeds in one shell and 1 teaspoon herb seeds in the other. Then, add a bit more soil to each. Prop each eggshell in its stand.

❯ **Add a bit of water to each shell, but don't let the soil get too soaked.** Place the eggheads in a sunny location. Keep the soil moist. Seeds sprout quickly, so the eggheads will show green "hair" in about a week. How did the different seeds compare?

Try This!

Plants are outta this world! How in the universe do astronauts on the International Space Station farm in the final frontier? Explore NASA's video. Discover the way astronauts sprout plants in the weightlessness of space.

🔎 ScienceCasts vegetables in space

Chapter 5

ADAPTATIONS
ARE A MATTER OF LIFE AND DEATH

Along with a diversity of plants, Earth enjoys an amazing abundance of animal life. Animals have adapted for survival in all kinds of unique environments. They adapt by developing physical or behavioral **traits** that help them to stay alive and reproduce.

Adaptation is a matter of life and death. If animals did not adapt to their environments, they would die.

ESSENTIAL QUESTION

How is adaptation necessary for survival?

Physical traits are related to the body. Owls, for example, are adapted with powerful **talons** that pierce their prey's skulls. These talons can mean the difference between death and survival.

BACKYARD BIOLOGY

WORDS TO KNOW

trait: a characteristic.

talon: a claw belonging to a bird of prey.

tundra: a treeless Arctic region that is permanently frozen below the top layer of soil.

reptile: a cold-blooded animal such as a snake, lizard, alligator, or turtle that has a spine, lays eggs, has scales or horny places, and breathes air.

Behavioral traits are a certain way of acting. The hognose snake rolls over, shows its belly, and plays dead in order to baffle predators, such as hawks. The snake even hangs out its tongue for dramatic effect!

Because environments vary greatly, adaptations do too. Do you live in the steamy Florida Everglades? You don't expect to spy an Arctic fox slinking through the swamps. The Arctic fox is a mammal and a member of the dog family that lives in cold regions. A predator of voles and lemmings and prey to snowy owls and polar bears, the fox adapts to winter by transforming its light, brownish-gray summer coat into a lush, white coat. The coat is the fox's way of camouflaging itself. This helps the Arctic fox hunt rodents and dodge a predator's choppers!

In bitter winds and blinding blizzards, the Arctic fox tunnels deep into snow. It hunkers in these burrows for shelter from storms. Which is the physical adaptation and which is behavioral?

Dead or alive?

Credit: Prime Hook National Wildlife Refuge (CC BY 2.0)

Do you live in Alaska's **tundra**? You don't expect to encounter an armor-plated alligator there. This giant **reptile** grows more than 11 feet long and weighs as much as a ton. It has adapted for survival in the intense sunshine and heat of the Florida Everglades.

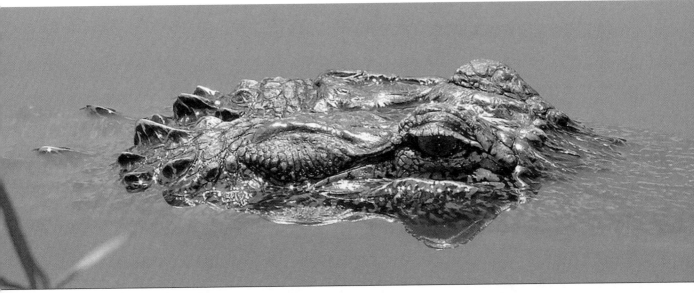

Hard at work hunting

Motionless alligators spy on prey with eyes that peer out just above the surface of marshy waters. When unsuspecting prey, such as a swimming turtle or a flying gull, comes within range, the predator quickly attacks. It can even grab a raccoon scuttling up a swooping tree limb. The alligator lunges five feet into the air to snatch prey and swallow it whole.

An alligator's fierce JAWS, packed with about 80 razor-sharp TEETH, smash mammal, bird, and fish bones. These powerhouse jaws can destroy reptile shells.

Around the World

Every environment enjoys its own unique characteristics. Do you live in a tropical place such as Honolulu, Hawaii? The temperature probably doesn't change much. As the American city with the least seasonal change, Honolulu's average temperature is 77 degrees Fahrenheit (25 degrees Celsius). Perhaps you live in an area that experiences dramatic seasonal changes and a wide range of temperatures. How do you adapt as winter sweeps in? Maybe you bundle up in layers and yank on mittens and toasty boots to explore snowy environments. How do animals adapt to seasonal changes where you live? As you observe animals in the wild, notice physical and behavioral traits that help them survive.

defense mechanism: a way to protect oneself.

endangered: a plant or animal species with a dangerously low population.

warren: a burrow where rabbits live.

mesmerize: to hold the attention of a person or people (or an animal) as if in a trance.

scavenger: an animal, bird, or insect that eats rotting food or animals that are already dead.

PREDATOR-PREY RELATIONSHIPS

Predator-prey relationships keep Earth's ecosystems thriving. They maintain balance among incredibly diverse species. Let's look at both sides of the equation.

Predators are always on the lookout for meat. They are adapted to hunt and kill for survival. Prey, on the other hand, are equipped with **defense mechanisms** to avoid ending up in a predator's jaws.

Consider the **endangered** Florida panther and the white-tailed deer, examples of predator and prey. A solitary carnivore, the panther slinks through swamplands while the tufts of fur and webbed skin between its toes muffle the sound. Add motion-detecting whiskers, a keen sense of smell, stellar night vision, and swiveling ears that zone in on a deer rustling through the brush, and you have a perfect predator.

The Performing Stoat

The stoat is a sleek-bodied member of the weasel family. It lives in Europe, New Zealand, and North America. Small and energetic, the predator takes down prey 10 times its size with a bizarre hunting strategy! Outside rabbit **warrens**, this carnivore dances. The stoat twists, twirls, and boings into the air! Curious rabbits pop out of hiding to watch the acrobatic show. Suddenly, the stoat pounces, killing a **mesmerized** rabbit with one swift bite to the throat.

Watch the acrobatic stoat perform its deadly dance to hypnotize prey.

🔎 Nat Geo deadliest stoat

Credit: U.S. Fish and Wildlife Services (CC BY 2.0)

Taking down large prey is hazardous for a panther—deer have sharp hooves. The carnivore relies on a quick kill. Sharp fangs pierce the deer's neck. Strong teeth rip at the meat. A tongue covered with horny tips cuts like scissors. After feeding, the panther drags the carcass under a tree. It heaps leaves and dirt over leftovers to conceal them from **scavengers**. The panther will return for future meals.

The **PANTHER is ADAPTED** to hunt animals and devour meat. The **MAGNIFICENT** big cat reigns at the top of the Everglades **FOOD CHAIN**.

But, sometimes, the predator isn't successful. The fleet-footed white-tailed deer is adapted with speed and leaping skills to avoid the panther's attack. As the panther lunges, the agile deer bounds on long legs over an 8-foot tree trunk and tears through swamplands at 40 miles per hour.

WORDS TO KNOW

projectile vomit: a sudden and strong barfing that causes the vomit to travel some distance.

acidic: from acids, which are chemical compounds that taste sour, bitter, or tart. Examples are vinegar and lemon juice. Water also contains some acid.

The deer is also a skilled swimmer. It jumps into deep water to throw the predator off its scent. Confused, the panther gives up. It whiffs the scent of an armadillo and slinks away to find a not-so-favorite meal.

UNUSUAL ANIMAL DEFENSES

Woodlice eat **SCAT**. That's poop and animal droppings! Woodlice recycle scat straight back into the soil.

In the wild, it's all about survival. How do prey keep from becoming dinner? Some defenses are just a bit gross.

For example, the fulmar is a seabird native to Newfoundland, the British Isles, and the Arctic Circle. It resembles a gull. In fact, fulmar means "foul gull." No wonder. It's adapted with an interesting defense—vomit! When threatened, the fulmar **projectile-vomits** an oily, fishy glop on its enemies. Bright orange goop smacks predators as far as 5 feet away. The reeking stuff isn't only gross—it's also dangerous. The **acidic** vomit can damage the waterproof coating on an enemy's feathers.

The hagfish is a nearly blind, eel-like fish. A scavenger that feasts on rotting flesh from dead fish, it lives in oceans around the globe. The hagfish has a jawless mouth with two sets of teeth, circled by tentacles. Swimming underwater, the hagfish looks like easy pickings for sharks. But it's packing a creepy defense. Slime!

Explore protective puking in a Gross Science video. How do other animals launch this defense?

🔍 Gross Science vomiting

PS

Gators Are Prehistoric!

Although other predators evolved through the ages, alligators remain untouched. A ferocious top predator, the alligator is a survivor.

Evan Whiting of Minnesota studies relationships between reptiles and their environments through time. Through fossil records, he discovered that today's alligators are the same species as their fossil ancestors.

Whiting noted, "If we could step back in time 8 million years, you'd basically see the same animal crawling around then as you would see today. . . . Even 30 million years ago, they didn't look much different."

WORDS TO KNOW

venomous: poisonous.

overwinter: to last through the winter.

antifreeze: a liquid that is added to a second liquid to lower the temperature at which the second liquid freezes.

stockpile: to store large amounts of something for later use. Also called hoarding.

hibernate: to sleep through the winter in a cave or underground.

migration: the seasonal movement of animals from one place to another.

What happens when a shark clamps its huge jaws on the hagfish? Thick slime oozes from hundreds of pores on the fish's body. The slime swirls into a gooey "cocoon" that surrounds the hagfish. In seconds, gunky slime clogs the fierce predator's gills. The suffocating shark retreats.

But how does the hagfish escape its own slimy clutches? With an amazing rope trick! It ties itself into a knot. The fish shivers the knot down its thin body all the way to its tail as it wrings the gunk away.

The Texas horned lizard is less than 3 inches long, but it has very powerful defenses. The lizard resembles a mini dragon with a scaly body spiked with prickly thorns. This armor is great camouflage in deserts, and makes the lizard tricky for hungry bobcats, coyotes, or snakes to eat.

But that's not all. This tiny reptile squirts blood out of miniature blood vessels in its bulging eyes. As if blood isn't nasty enough, it's flavored with poisonous chemicals, probably because of the horned lizard's favorite snack—**venomous** ants! Blinded and baffled by vile squirting blood, most predators run away. Wouldn't you?

Watch the horny lizard's blood-spraying adaptation in action!

🔍 Nat Geo horned lizard

PS

Some **INSECTS,** including beetles and midges, hang around during **COLD WINTERS.** They overwinter with physical **ADAPTATIONS.** Water moves out of their body's cells into spaces between the cells. Some scientists call this "biological **antifreeze!"**

SEASONAL ADAPTATIONS

Do you live in a place that has cold winters? What do you see as the cold weather approaches? You might spot chipmunks hoarding their secret stashes. Chipmunks **stockpile** nuts and acorns to survive lean times. Other animals handle winter by **hibernating**. Imagine a bear all cozy and warm in its den, sleeping through the long, cold winter.

Some animals escape bitter temperatures and icy snows with another behavioral adaptation—**migration**. Monarch butterflies set off on marathon flights from the eastern and midwestern parts of the United States and flutter all the way to balmy climates in Guatemala, Honduras, and Mexico.

Just remember, wild animals are adapted for life in their own natural environments. They shouldn't be confined in cages, homes, and yards. In many areas, it's against the law to remove animals from habitats and raise them in captivity. We also don't want wild animals moved from one area to another, which can upset the natural balance and result in destroyed ecosystems. Please leave critters in their own homes. Keep wild animals wild!

ESSENTIAL QUESTION

How is adaptation necessary for survival?

HABITAT
OBSERVATION

You can learn a lot about animal adaptations by observing them in the wild. Try this activity to immerse yourself in the natural world around you!

❯ **Scout around for a habitat to observe.** You might select the edge of a pond, a wooded area, a park, or a decaying log. Quietly, without disturbing it, watch the ecosystem from both faraway and up-close perspectives. Start a scientific method worksheet in your science journal. Use a chart to record your observations.

❯ **What types of animals and plants live in the habitat?** What evidence of adaptations, such as stockpiling or hoarding, camouflage, and defense mechanisms, do you observe? How do living and non-living things interact?

❯ **Sketch the plants and animals you see in the ecosystem.** With an adult's help, head to the library to identify them.

Try This!

Revisit the ecosystem after a change of seasons or weather conditions. For example, observe it after a rainfall or snowfall. Explore it after significant changes, such as a controlled burn, tree planting, reseeding, or flooding. What similarities and differences do you notice?

Two Heads Are Better Than One!

In September 2018, a person in Woodbridge, Virginia, encountered a strange backyard visitor. A double-headed venomous copperhead snake! Extremely rare, this **bicephalic** beast was just a baby. It faced a brief lifespan in the wild. **Herpetologist** John Kleopfer and his team at the Wildlife Center of Virginia studied the two-headed wonder. Through **radiographs**, they determined the copperhead's body shared one heart and one set of lungs. But it relied on both heads for eating. The right side was more developed and better at processing food, but the left side contained the dominant **esophagus**.

Watch this snake in action!

🔎 ABC two-headed

WORDS TO KNOW

bicephalic: having two heads.

herpetologist: a scientist who studies reptiles and amphibians.

radiograph: an image produced by X-rays or other forms of radiation.

esophagus: the long tube connecting the mouth to the stomach.

FANTANIMAL

How are animals adapted for life where you live? Get some ideas for a new kind of animal from different adaptations around the world!

❯ **What physical and behavioral adaptations do animals need to survive in your environment?** Are they adapted with camouflage to fool predators? Do they have special ears or eyes for hunting? Think about adaptations you find fascinating.

❯ **Let your imagination run wild! Imagine what your area would be like with completely different conditions,** such as year-round ice, midnight sun, or **fluorescent** trees.

Sloths are adapted to a life spent hanging in branches with long, clingy fingernails and hair that grows toward the front so rain flows right off!
Credit: Christian Mehlführer (CC BY 2.5)

❯ **Sketch your fantanimal** and include real and imagined adaptations for survival in your environment's new conditions.

❯ **To decorate your animal, select items to glue on it,** such as art paper, beads, buttons, cotton balls, fabric swatches, feathers, glitter, sequins, shells. Add other odds and ends you have available. Create a model of your fantanimal.

Think About It!

As temperatures rise, **precipitation** patterns change, and weather becomes increasingly unpredictable, animals must move, adapt, or die. What happens to animals that can't adapt to climate change? Research the impact of climate change on animal life.

WORDS TO KNOW

fluorescent: a bright color that seems to reflect light.

precipitation: water in the air in any form, such as snow, hail, or rain, that falls to the ground.

ANIMAL TRACKER
PLASTER CASTER

Which wild animals share your environment? Sometimes, you can hear them, but other times, night animals are silent. Try this!

Caution: Ask an adult to help you cut the bottle into rings and scout for tracks. Wear a life vest near water.

> **Choose a squishy area to explore,** preferably a place where animals drink water. You might choose a pond, creek, or stream, or even a large mud puddle. Riverbanks and sandbars work well, too.

> **It's tricky to locate a clear track in the wild.** Animals are on the move and tracks get smudged. Scout for a deep track that contains a strong imprint all the way around. Study the track. Is it webbed? Does it include claws? Tail or wing imprints? Perhaps the animal left behind a bit of fur, a quill, or a feather. Lightly brush away any **debris**, such as twigs, stones, and leaves. Don't use too much force or it will smear the track.

> **Cut the bottle into 2-inch ringed sections.** Center one ring over the track. Carefully press the ring about ½ inch into the ground. Now you have a form to hold the plaster of Paris in place.

> **Pour a cup of water into the small bucket.** Slowly sprinkle plaster of Paris into the bucket, following the directions on the carton. Build the plaster to a peak about a half inch over the top of the water. Let the mixture stand in the bucket for several minutes.

WORDS TO KNOW

debris: pieces of dead plants or branches.

❯ **After the plaster of Paris has absorbed some of the water, slowly stir the mixture.** This is the trickiest step! Keep stirring until the plaster has no lumps and has a smooth, creamy consistency. Stir very slowly to avoid creating air bubbles. Air bubbles result in a less detailed cast. To release any bubbles that do form, carefully rap the bottom of the bucket against a tree stump, rock, or other hard surface. Any air bubbles will rise to the top. Continue rapping until bubbles stop rising.

❯ **Pour some plaster into the ring— to the side of the track—to make the cast.** Let the plaster ooze over the track on its own and then add more plaster to fill the ring to the top. Avoid pouring plaster directly onto the track, or you may not get a good casting.

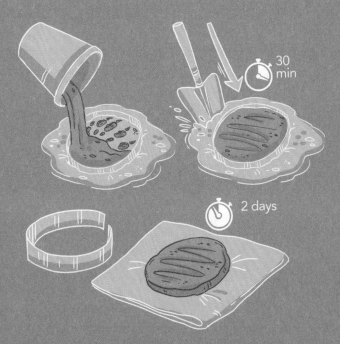

❯ **Allow the cast to harden completely.** Depending on weather conditions, it may take 30 to 60 minutes. In the meantime, scout for other tracks. Can you identify the critters that left them?

❯ **When the plaster is hard, use a garden trowel or shovel to push aside the soil about 5 inches outside the cast.** Then, dig away beneath the cast. Gently lift out the cast. If it doesn't come out, carefully place it back in position. Remove more earth. It might be tempting to try to jack up the cast with the shovel or a stick. But the cast is very fragile. Try to lift it gently with your hands so the cast doesn't crack or crumble. Use scissors to cut away the plastic ring.

❯ **Wrap the fragile cast in newspaper or bubble wrap to cushion it until you get home.** Then, allow it to thoroughly dry for two days. As it dries, the cast will feel warm when you touch it. When it feels cool, you can clean the cast.

Try This!

Check out the North American Animal Tracking database to explore the images skilled trackers share.

🔍 North American Animal Tracking database

Have you spotted similar tracks in your own environment?

ROLY-POLY
HABITAT IN A BOX

Woodlice are tiny, armored decomposers that look like insects. They have many nicknames that make them sound like bugs— roly-poly bugs, doodlebugs, armadillo bugs, potato or pill bugs—but woodlice are actually crustaceans with seven pairs of legs. They are adapted with physical and behavioral defenses that include a hard, outer skeleton with plates that cover their bodies like armor. When threatened or touched, woodlice curl into tight, protective balls.

BIO BOX
° garden gloves
° plastic box with lid
° soil
° mulch
° oats
° large leaves
° small plastic tub with lid
° shovel or trowel
° science journal

Where can you unearth woodlice? They love soil and moisture. Scout under leaf litter, decaying plant matter, and grass clippings. They hang out in the dark under stacks of wood, piles of mulch, and clay pots, too. You can build a temporary home for a roly-poly and observe its behaviors before you release it back into its natural environment.

> **Wear garden gloves and fill the plastic box about halfway with moist soil.** Save some soil for the next step. Spread a layer of mulch, such as chopped up leaves, straw, or grass clippings, over the soil. Sprinkle a layer of oats over the mulch. Cover the top with large leaves. This will be the habitat for your woodlice.

> **In the small tub, layer moist soil and small leaves.** This will be the container to transport the roly-polies.

> **Trek outdoors to scout for roly-polies.** Wear gloves and use a shovel or garden trowel to turn over leaves and piles of twigs. Carefully flip rocks and lift logs. When you find some roly-polies, gently place them in the transporter. In your science journal, note the location where you found the roly-polies, so you can return them to the same place in several days.

WORDS TO KNOW

crustacean: a type of animal, such as a crab or lobster, that lives mainly in water. It has several pairs of legs and its body is made up of sections covered in a hard outer shell.

❯ **Gently transfer roly-polies into the habitat you prepared for them.** Allow them to burrow into the layers and close the lid. Observe the roly-polies for several days. Keep the soil moist and sprinkle some oats and mulch into the habitat. Start a scientific method worksheet in your science journal. What do you think the roly-polies will spend their time doing? Will they move around a lot? Will they group together or stay separate? Record your observations and create illustrations to describe their activities and behaviors.

❯ **After the observation period, return all the roly-polies to their natural environment.** Wear gloves as you gently remove layers in the habitat to unearth the critters. Place them into a fresh transporter. Then, carefully release them where you found them.

Try This!

Watch this PBS video about roly-polies. What makes it a crustacean rather than an insect? How did it evolve from life in the sea?

🔎 PBS roly-polies

Chapter 6

ANIMAL
LIFE CYCLES

Just as with plants, the life cycle for animals is an essential part of survival of the species. Animals are born and they go through stages of development as they grow into adults. From **larva** to yellow jacket. From tadpole to frog. From egg to emu. From kit to honey badger. As adults, animals reproduce and replace themselves with new generations. In time, they die.

ESSENTIAL QUESTION

Why is reproduction critical for a species' survival?

Animals accomplish reproduction much differently from plants, as you might suspect! Animals are born with a mating **instinct**, a natural behavior or characteristic. Mating allows animals to produce **offspring** of their own kind. This is how a species survives and the circle of life keeps rolling.

Nature Detective

Some animals, including birds, reptiles, **amphibians**, insects, and fish, are **oviparous**. They lay eggs that hatch into offspring outside the mother's body. Other animals, such as most mammals, are **viviparous**. They bear live offspring.

Through **sexual reproduction**, adult animals pass **genes** onto their offspring. Babies inherit certain characteristics from each of their parents, which pass on from one generation to the next.

How does sexual reproduction take place? Female and male animals produce sex cells. Females produce egg cells. Males produce sperm cells. Through fertilization, or the union of male and female reproductive cells, the egg begins to develop. It changes and grows into a baby.

A honey badger and her baby

Credit: Derek Keats (CC BY 2.0)

BACKYARD BIOLOGY

Some animal adaptations are very unusual! Watch this mating ritual among the grouse. Why might they have evolved to do this?

🔍 Nat Geo grouse mating

PS

ATTRACTING A MATE

Before reproducing, animals compete to attract mates. They engage in mating **rituals**. For example, male peacocks strut and show off shimmery tail plumage to dazzle females. Male fiddler crabs waggle enlarged claws to entice females—and warn rivals to scram! Adapted for nightlife with **bioluminescence**, fireflies flash lights in a special pattern.

Fireflies at night

Credit: Derek Keats (CC BY 2.0) Mike Lewinski (CC BY 2.0)

Competition is often ferocious. Some animals, including moose, battle for a partner. One-ton males, called bulls, clash for females, called cows. Two grunting, snorting bulls smash and slam huge, branched antlers together. They keep fighting until one battered fighter hustles away. Then, the victor claims his mate.

Some **FEMALES** are cannibals! Female black widow spiders, jumping spiders, and praying mantises sometimes **KILL AND GOBBLE** their partners after mating.

APPARENTLY, PRAYING MANTIS FEMALES SOMETIMES KILL THE MALE AFTER MATING.

ANIMALS CAN GET PRETTY AGGRESSIVE WHEN IT COMES TO RELATIONSHIPS IN THE WILD.

I'M GLAD HUMAN RELATIONSHIPS AREN'T AS CRAZY!

SOMETIMES, WHEN MY DAD DOESN'T PICK UP HIS SOCKS, MY MOM SURE LOOKS LIKE SHE'S READY TO BITE HIS HEAD OFF....

WORDS TO KNOW

rutting season: the mating time of some animals.

krill: small crustaceans found in all the world's oceans.

Female warriors tussle, too. "Chir-lee, chir-lee!" That's the call of an Eastern bluebird. Scrappy females are extremely aggressive. They fight not only over mates, but also over prime nesting sites. Using its short beak as a weapon, one female might peck another to death.

Not all males and females reproduce. Only certain males and females win the opportunity to mate. Male Mormon crickets are fussy. They turn away females with lighter weights and choose heavier ones. It makes good sense for them! Heavier females bear more offspring, which means they produce more Mormon crickets.

Rutting season is an animal's mating time. During rutting season on a quiet neighborhood street near Anchorage, Alaska, a moose brawl broke out right in a family's driveway! **Watch the video to get in on the action.**

🔍 Nat Geo moose fight

Credit: Joel Herzberg, Bureau of Land Management (CC BY 2.0)

NATURAL SELECTION

Why is competition for mates so fierce? It's essential for reproduction. When animals fail to win mates, they don't reproduce. What happens when animals don't reproduce? They don't pass genetic traits to a new generation. They are unable to affect future generations of their species. In the example of the Mormon cricket, if heavier crickets are passing on genes, their offspring are likely to be heavy, too.

Climate Change Corner

Adélie penguins, averaging just 8.5 pounds, are among our planet's hardiest species. The most southerly breeding birds on Earth, they live in an extreme environment. Adults travel ashore to breed in summer months and lay eggs in nests built of stones. Parents take turns tending the eggs. They keep them warm and protected from predators that swoop down from the skies. When the babies hatch, they are nearly helpless. They depend on their parents for warmth, food, and protection. The adults endure epic struggles, traveling between 30 and 75 miles a day to find **krill** to eat and regurgitate into their chicks' mouths. But on Petrels Island in Antarctica, climate change proved devastating for a colony of 18,000 Adélie penguin breeding pairs. The adults were forced to swim longer distances to find food, leaving the babies alone for longer periods of time. In 2017, thousands of tiny chicks starved to death or froze. Only two chicks survived.

With a friend or family member, read this news article that explores the problem and what scientists are trying to do about it. What might the failure of chicks to survive mean for the species' future? What changes can people make to protect the species?

🔎 Guardian penguin breeding

Watch this amazing 360-degree movie to take a trip to an Adélie penguin breeding colony on Antarctica's Gardener Island.

🔎 360 video Adelie

BACKYARD BIOLOGY

WORDS TO KNOW

natural selection: one of the basic means of evolution in which organisms that are well-adapted to their environment are better able to survive, reproduce, and pass along their useful traits to offspring.

DNA: deoxyribonucleic acid. The substance found in your cells that carries your genes, the genetic information that contains the blueprint of who you are.

chromosome: the part of a cell that contains genes.

genetic basis: genes that are beneficial for offspring to inherit.

Charles Darwin (1809–1882) was a naturalist who wrote a book called *On the Origin of Species*. According to Darwin's theory of **natural selection**, animals best adapted for survival in their environments win chances to reproduce. They pass along beneficial traits to the next generation. Some of those offspring survive, reproduce, and carry on the cycle.

Made of the **CHEMICAL DNA (deoxyribonucleic acid), chromosomes** contain GENES that give living things their characteristics. DNA, in the form of a double pair of twisted strands that look like a crooked ladder, is an important messenger. It carries GENETIC information from **one generation to the next.**

As Mormon crickets continue to evolve, what kind of natural selection might occur? Lighter females might continue to lose mating wars. Only heavier females could be the ones to reproduce. Why? The trait—greater weight—has a **genetic basis**. It's an advantage for the future of the species. Heavier females lay more eggs. They bear more offspring, including heavier female babies. As time passes, greater numbers of heavier females might become more common.

Now that we've looked at lots of different plants and animals and the ways they struggle to survive, let's think more about what we as individuals can do to protect them.

ESSENTIAL QUESTION

Why is reproduction critical for a species' survival?

FINE-FEATHERED
FRIENDS

BIO BOX
° garden gloves
° plastic containers
° collection bag
° science journal and pencil

Birds build nests where they lay and hatch eggs and where offspring can grow. Collect twigs, pine needles, moss, dandelion fluff, feathers, mud, and other natural elements to build a nest that will attract birds!

> **Spend time looking around to discover where birds build nests.** Please avoid disturbing nesting birds. When exploring, wear garden gloves and gather materials to build your nest. Store mud in plastic containers and place materials in a collection bag.

> **Consider the type of nest to build.** Create a scientific method worksheet in your science journal to help you plan. Do some research. What species will hatch in your nest? Which building materials does the species prefer? How heavy and secure will the nest need to be?

The fierce harpy eagle is the largest raptor in the rainforest, with a wingspan of more than 7 feet and talons that span 7 inches. The top predator snatches howler monkeys to carry back to ravenous chicks waiting in its nest.

> **Locate a low-slung, forked tree branch.** Using only your hands and natural elements, build a nest in the fork. Use mud to pack building materials together. It's not easy. But many birds do the job with only their beaks!

> **Test the nest.** Place pebbles inside to represent eggs. Is the nest strong enough to support them? What adjustments can you make to build a sturdier nest?

Try This!

Visit the Cornell Lab of Ornithology's NestWatch website. Discover how you can become part of a nationwide program. You'll monitor a nesting area, collect data, and share observations. Create your own account and take a code of conduct quiz to get started.

Cornell Lab of Ornithology's NestWatch

METAMORPHO-PLATE

Complete **metamorphosis** is a series of changes many organisms go through as they develop. Through physical changes, the newborn and the adult look nothing alike. Babies that go through a complete metamorphosis are total transformers! Create a life cycle model that illustrates transformation from egg to monarch butterfly.

❯ **Make a circle of change.** Cut a sheet of colored paper into a circle that fits the inner section of a large paper plate. Fold the circle in half. Firmly press the edge between your fingers. Fold it in half again. Press the second edge.

❯ **Unfold and flatten the circle.** You should see four pie-slice sections. Use a permanent marker to trace over the fold lines. Glue the paper in the center of the plate. Hold the paper flat until it sticks.

❯ **On the plate's rim, label four sections:** Egg, Caterpillar, Chrysalis, Butterfly.

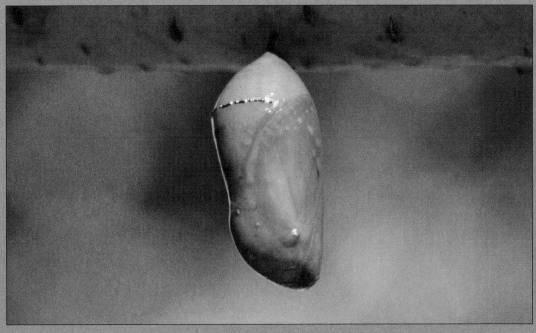

> **Time for the egg!** Glue one piece of orzo onto a leaf. As the orzo dries, glue a twig in the Egg section. Then, glue the leaf with the orzo so it hangs from the twig.

> **The next stage is the caterpillar.** Glue one piece of rotini in the center of another leaf. Make a twig perch, and glue it in place in the Caterpillar section.

> **The caterpillar morphed into a chrysalis!** Glue another twig into the Chrysalis section. Glue the conchiglie so it hangs from the twig.

> **When metamorphosis is complete, the butterfly emerges!** Glue a flower into the Butterfly section. Place the farfalle in flight over it.

Try This!

Watch this incredible video of monarch metamorphosis. How does the caterpillar shed its skin to transform?

🔎 monarch metamorphosis time lapse

WORDS TO KNOW

metamorphosis: an animal's complete change in physical form as it develops into an adult.

97

Chapter 7

BE THE
DIFFERENCE

LITTLE ACTIONS MATTER MORE THAN EVER.

HERE ARE SMALL THINGS YOU CAN DO TO HELP:

REDUCE YOUR PLASTIC WASTE! USE REUSABLE CONTAINERS AND WRAPS AT LUNCH.

PLANT NATIVE FLOWERS TO HELP POLLINATORS.

GROW YOUR OWN FOOD IN YOUR BACKYARD!

SAY NO THANKS TO SINGLE-USE PLASTICS AT RESTAURANTS AND FAST-FOOD CHAINS.

YOU CAN BRING YOUR OWN REUSABLE CONTAINERS INSTEAD!

Earth's enormous circle of life links all living things together in interconnected cycles, where our actions might launch a chain of events that can harm living things. In your own outdoor investigations, you've probably noticed the impact on the environment that people have made.

Have you seen plastic bags billowing like ghosts from jam-packed trash cans? Maybe you've spotted gnarled fishing line, crushed bait containers, and squashed plastic bottles bobbing in a lake or on a beach? Have you seen a single boot or flipflop left under a picnic table? Our actions impact not only the environments right outside our doors, but they can also hurt an ecosystem's entire food chain and reach ecosystems far away.

ESSENTIAL QUESTION

How do our actions impact the environment?

POLLUTANTS THROUGH THE FOOD CHAIN

Bioaccumulation is the buildup of harmful substances inside the tissue of living things. Because living things are connected through food chains, this buildup gets passed along. Plus, the buildup increases as it goes. Through **biomagnification**, harmful substances become more concentrated as they move up a food chain. We can see this happening in an ocean ecosystem. Take a look at an example.

First, hazardous chemicals leak into the environment from a nearby processing plant. They ooze onto land, **contaminating** beaches. They seep into water, spreading pollution.

Litter washed up on a beach in Hawaii
Credit: Ian Kirk (CC BY 2.0)

99

WORDS TO KNOW

remote: faraway and isolated.

Plankton, the first link in marine food chains, soak up these chemicals. Shrimp nibble plankton and take in chemicals stored in the plankton's tissues. Next, a cuttlefish devours the shrimp. A shark eats the cuttlefish. The toxic buildups increase. Chemicals move through the chain, growing more intense at each level.

Watch this astonishing video of a diver rescuing an enormous whale shark tangled in deadly fishing line! What did you find surprising about the rescue?

🔍 Smithsonian whale shark diver

What happens when an ENDANGERED sea turtle spots a plastic bag bobbing in waves? The turtle might mistake the bag for a JELLYFISH, its favorite dinner, and gobble it up. Sadly, the bag can block the sea turtle's digestive tract and kill the turtle.

Credit: Ian Kirk (CC BY 2.0)

Killing the Young

Our actions can impact living things thousands of miles from where we live. Photographers David Liittschwager and Susan Middleton wrote *Archipelago: Portraits of Life in the World's Most Remote Island Sanctuary.* While researching their book, they visited **remote** coral reefs in the Hawaiian Islands. There, they made friends with a young albatross named Shed Bird that still lived in its mother's nest. Soon, the seabird would be heading out of the nest, soaring over the sea, and taking care of itself. But before that could happen, Shed Bird died.

His parents, swooping over waves to snag squid for mealtimes, also ate the rubbish floating in the water. From the sky, bits of balloons, broken toys, disposable lighters, and bottle caps looked like food—so the hungry birds ate the trash. When the parents regurgitated food to feed their baby, Shed Bird also swallowed the debris. The young albatross died from human garbage.

A healthy albatross in flight

Where does all this trash come from? Maybe it fluttered out of a recycling truck. Winds blew it miles away. Perhaps someone accidentally kicked a plastic spoon into a storm grate or carelessly dropped a plastic water bottle at the beach.

You might think ONE PIECE OF LITTER doesn't matter. But all the bits of **TRASH** add up to so much garbage that it's **CLOGGING** our oceans.

KIDS TAKE ACTION

Brazil's Amazon rainforests are blazing. Sea levels are rising. With no salmon to eat in Canada, grizzly bears are starving. Greenland's ice sheets are melting. Folks in subarctic Iceland lost the once-gigantic Okjökull Glacier to climate change and held a funeral to commemorate the loss.

Our home—Earth—is on fire. Kids know this is not a drill. It's an emergency.

Greta Thunberg leads School Strike for Climate Change

MORE SMALL THINGS YOU CAN DO TO HELP:

BUY SECOND-HAND CLOTHING. THE TEXTILE INDUSTRY IS A HUGE POLLUTER.

FIX, REPAIR, RESELL, DONATE, OR TRADE ITEMS. MAKE THE GARBAGE CAN A LAST OPTION!

OUR "I'LL JUST BUY A NEW ONE" MINDSET IS CREATING EXTRA WASTE WE DON'T NEED.

GET INVOLVED WITH GREEN INITIATIVE PROGRAMS IN YOUR AREA.

In September 2019, days before world leaders gathered at the United Nations Climate Summit, kids in more than a thousand cities across the world united in the same goal. They urgently tackled the fight of their lives: Their futures.

In historic, youth-lead demonstrations, millions of young people hit the streets during School Strike For Climate Change. Kids skipped school and walked out of jobs to protest. From Mumbai, India, to Washington, DC., kids presented passionate speeches, waved signs, and chanted together. They demanded governments take urgent action to prevent continued global warming and climate change. Protestors implored world leaders to decrease dependency on fossil fuels and reduce carbon emissions.

In 2019, Greta Thunberg was named the *Time* Person of the Year! She is the youngest person ever to receive this honor. Read the article about it here.

🔎 Time Greta Thunberg

Swedish teen Greta Thunberg inspired Fridays For Future, or School Strike For Climate Change. In 2018, Greta, then 15, created signs to advocate for urgent action and spent two weeks "on strike" outside Swedish Parliament. Since then, she has conducted a strike each Friday. The movement continues to gain worldwide momentum.

WORDS TO KNOW

tsunami: a very large ocean wave, usually caused by an earthquake.

KEEP IT ROLLING!

Nature shares its gifts with us. It provides everything we need to survive, grow, change, and flourish. You've been exploring the nature around you, and now it's time to think about how you can give back to nature. It's easy to think of the plants, animals, water, air, and other resources as limitless, but they will all run out if we don't take care of our planet. What can you do to help?

Perhaps you can select an area of a park or playground and clear garbage regularly. Pitch in to clean up a creek or pond. Clear invasive plants from a nearby natural area. Rally friends to plant trees. Organize a litter-free lunch. Reduce your farm-to-plate "food miles." Those are distances that food is transported from producers, such as farmers, to consumers, or folks who purchase and eat it.

Cleaning up the beach
Credit: Airman 1st Class Sadie Colbert

Traveling Trash

The devastating earthquake and **tsunami** that hit Japan in March 2011 killed nearly 16,000 people and left more than 500,000 homeless. And it swept about 20 million tons of debris into the Pacific Ocean. The debris from the tsunami could have a major impact on wildlife. Televisions, washing machines, refrigerators, and other appliances floating in the water carry harmful chemicals. By September 2015, 64 pieces of the tsunami's debris meandered through the vast Pacific Ocean to faraway places across the planet, including Hawaii, Alaska, California, and British Columbia! Among the floating debris was a Harley-Davidson motorcycle with a Japanese serial number, found on Graham Island in Vancouver, British Columbia, Canada.

Read a news article to discover what wreckage survived the devastation. Which items were returned to their owners? And where is that motorcycle today?

🔎 BBC News tsunami debris

Foods that are processed and moved long distances with planes, trains, and trucks use fossil fuels that impact the climate. Some foods require refrigeration. Others must be frozen for safe transport. Both increase energy costs.

Use your knowledge of biology to grow your own fresh and nutritious foods—locally. If you have a backyard or rooftop growing area, you might create a small vegetable garden to tend with family and friends. Try planting carrots, radishes, green beans, lettuce, and cherry tomatoes. They grow quickly and are relatively easy to maintain. You can even grow your own herbs and veggies in windowsill planters. No matter where your space, observe the ways your plants sprout, grow, and change.

Imagine the impact you'll make. It's for your future, your planet's future, and for the circle of life.

ESSENTIAL QUESTION

How do our actions impact the environment?

ORGANIZE A
CLEANUP!

Just one person makes a difference in protecting living things. Imagine the impact a group can make! Select an outdoor area, such as a nature trail, forest preserve, or creek. Develop a plan to work with others to spruce it up.

Caution: Don't forget to get permission from city officials, park services, or private owners before you start.

❯ **Plan!** Rally friends, family, and your community. Encourage people to protect, defend, and restore nature with a cleanup. Set a date and time for the event.

❯ **Publicize!** Design clever, colorful flyers and posters you can hang. Use social media to spread the word. If you're part of a school blog, post "before" photos from the cleanup site. Host a podcast to rally others and share information through video platforms such as Snapchat. Contact a local news group to write an article about the cleanup.

❯ **Gather supplies!** Ask for donations of cleaning supplies, such as leaf and yard waste recycling bags and garbage bags. Collect tongs for picking up sharp items and rubber and gardening gloves to protect hands.

❯ **Clean up!** Greet volunteers and thank them for joining you. Ask volunteers to be aware of broken bottles and other sharp materials they shouldn't touch. As everyone cleans, set aside recyclables, including bottles, cans, and newspapers, to take to a recycling center. Collect trash in bags for disposal. Don't forget to clear away your own trash!

Try This!

Visit the EPA's website to learn where site-specific cleanups are taking place in your community. You can search by street address, city, state, and more. Then pitch in to help out.

⌕ EPA Cleanups

❯ **Debrief!** Afterward, evaluate the event. How many volunteers pitched in? What changes can improve the next cleanup? If you performed a podcast or wrote a blog, update it with "after" photos. Add action shots of enthusiastic volunteers. Congratulations on a job well done!

WETLAND PLANT
POLLUTION

BIO BOX
- science journal
- 2 fern plants
- stick-on labels
- ruler
- water
- cooking oil
- Epsom salt
- soil
- sand

Make predictions and compare results! Water one outdoor fern plant, a typical plant found in wetlands, with polluted water. Water a second with its runoff. How will pollutants impact growth?

❯ **Start a scientific method worksheet in your science journal.** Prepare two fern plants that are approximately the same size. With a permanent marker, write "Wetland 1" and "Wetland 2" on stick-on labels. Attach one label to each fern. Measure each plant's height and record the measurements on your worksheet. Write a description of each plant's health.

❯ **Place a saucer under each plant.** You'll use the saucers to collect runoff water later. If you have a camera, snap a "before" photo of each plant.

❯ **Pollute the water!** Fill an empty 2-liter bottle with tap water. Pour it into a bucket. Add ½ cup cooking oil and ¼ cup Epsom salt. Mix until salt dissolves. Add 1 cup of soil and sand mixed together and stir.

❯ **Each day for seven days, water Wetland 1 with the polluted mixture.** On day one, water Wetland 2 with tap water.

❯ **Starting with day two, water Wetland 2 with runoff water from the saucer of Wetland 1.** Predict what will happen through the week. Make notes in your journal to describe outcomes. Where do the oil and sediments collect? Which plant is affected first? Do your plants survive?

Try This!

After seven days, assess your findings. How does polluted water impact wetland plant growth? If you took a "before" picture, snap an "after" one. Compare images. If you encounter a plant that's parched and shriveled, is it really a goner? Read this journal article to learn about plant resuscitation.

🔎 gentle art of plant resuscitation

TEST BUTTERFLY
FEEDERS

Climate change has impacted the number of butterflies in the wild. Build two feeders and see how many butterflies come to hang out. You'll probably see plenty of other insects come to your feeders, too. Look them up in a field guide to identify them.

> **Caution:** Ask an adult for help with the hammer and nail and with boiling the sugar water.

> Combine 9 teaspoons of water and 1 teaspoon of sugar (use tablespoons for a larger jar) in a saucepan. Boil until the sugar is dissolved. Let the sugar water cool.

> **Use a hammer and nail** to make a small hole in the lid of the small jar.

> **Cut a strip of the kitchen sponge.** Pull it through the lid's hole, leaving about a half-inch sticking out from the top. The sponge must be a tight fit so liquid doesn't drip. Put water in the jar to test it. If it leaks, try a bigger piece of sponge.

> **Make a hanger.** Tie some string around the mouth of the jar. Cut two more lengths of string about 30 inches long. Tie the end of one string around the string tied around the jar's mouth. Attach the other end on the jar's opposite side to make a loop. Tie the second length of string across from the first in the same way. Use one more piece of string to tie the tops of the loops together. Now, turn the jar upside down. Make sure it hangs steadily.

Butterflies TASTE with their HIND FEET! Special taste receptors, or nerve endings, allow the insects to zone in on the perfect plant.

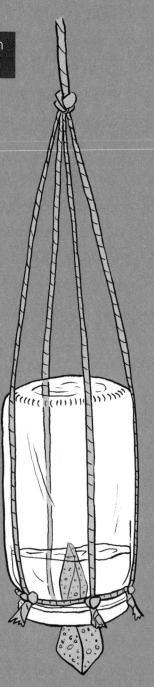

> **Decorate the jar with brightly colored construction paper** (flower shapes are best) or artificial flowers. The "prettier" it is, the more it will attract butterflies!

> **Fill the jar with the cooled sugar water.** Screw the lid on tightly. Turn the jar upside down. Hang your feeder outside and wait for butterflies to visit!

Butterfly Diet

A butterfly's tongue is specially adapted for a liquid diet. Called a **proboscis**, it is a built-in, tube-like tongue. It's like a straw! The butterfly uncoils the proboscis to suck up juicy nectar.

WORDS TO KNOW

proboscis: the sucking mouth part of honeybees and some other insects.

109

PLANT A
POLLINATOR GARDEN

The U.S. Fish & Wildlife Service reminds us, "Pollinators are the engine that runs healthy habitats." Yet, pollinators' numbers shrink as habitats change. Plant a pollinator garden to draw essential butterflies, bees, birds, beetles, and more.

❯ **Research plants that will thrive in your part of the country.** Consider wildflowers native to your region. Wildflowers are likely to be hearty and will require less maintenance. To select the appropriate seeds, bulbs, and small plants, visit National Wildlife Foundation's Native Plant Finder. Enter your zip code and explore your options.

🔎 National Wildlife Foundation's Native Plant Finder

❯ **Consider your local weather.** Is your area experiencing heavier rainfalls? Earlier freezes? Severe drought and frequent heat waves? Then, investigate your native soil. Is it well-drained? Clay-like, chalky, sandy? Which plants will most likely grow in the soil?

❯ **Choose a garden location.** Determine whether plants will best thrive in sunny, partially sunny, and shady locations. Consider how to provide wind protection for busy pollinators.

❯ **Prepare the soil for the garden bed.** Remove branches, rocks, dead leaves, etc. Turn over the soil with shovels, spading forks, and rakes. Work in at least one inch of organic matter or compost. Continue working the soil until you prepare a smooth surface.

❯ **Create your garden design.** Focus on plant colors and the sizes plants will reach at full bloom. How will you position plants so that smaller plants thrive among larger ones? How will you place plants according to varying amounts of sunlight required?

❯ **Follow the directions on seed and bulb packets and plant containers.** Thoroughly water the garden after planting. Make sure the soil is completely moistened. Watch the weather as time goes on to determine how much water your plants will need.

❯ **Watch changes through time.** Follow gardening's three w's: water, weed, and watch to nurture plants and welcome pollinators.

Try This!

Explore Michigan State's Pollinators and Protection site to boost your knowledge of pollinator-friendly habitats.

🔎 How to protect and increase pollinators

acidic: from acids, which are chemical compounds that taste sour, bitter, or tart. Examples are vinegar and lemon juice. Water also contains some acid.

adaptation: a change a plant or animal has made to help it survive.

adapt: to change to survive in new or different conditions.

algae: a simple organism found in water that is like a plant but without roots, stems, or leaves.

algae bloom: a rapid increase in an aquatic ecosystem's algae population.

amoebae: bloblike, single-celled organisms. Singular is amoeba.

amphibian: an animal with moist skin that is born in water but lives on land. An amphibian changes its body temperature by moving to warmer or cooler places. Frogs, toads, newts, efts, and salamanders are amphibians.

anatomy: the internal structure of an organism.

anther: the flower part that produces and holds pollen.

antibiotic overuse: using antibiotics when not needed.

antibodies: proteins that help the immune system fight infections or bacteria.

antifreeze: a liquid that is added to a second liquid to lower the temperature at which the second liquid freezes.

aquatic: living or growing in water.

arthritis: a medical condition that causes swollen joints, stiffness, and pain.

asexual: reproduction without male and female cells joining.

atmosphere: the mixture of gases surrounding a planet.

auxin: a chemical in a plant that causes leaves to bend and lengthen.

bacteria: single-celled organisms found in soil, water, plants, and animals. They help decay food. Some bacteria are harmful. Singular is bacterium.

bacteriologist: a scientist who studies bacteria.

bicephalic: having two heads.

bioaccumulation: the buildup of harmful substances inside the tissues of living things.

biologist: a scientist who studies biology.

biology: the study of life and of living organisms.

bioluminescence: the ability to create light from a chemical reaction inside an organism's body.

biomagnification: the process through which harmful substances become more concentrated as they pass up a food chain.

bog: a marshy wetland made of decomposing plants.

botany: the study of plants.

camouflage: the use of colors or patterns to blend in with a background.

cannibal: an animal that eats its own species.

carbohydrate: the sugar that is the source of food and energy in a plant.

carbon: an element that is found in all life on Earth and in coal, petroleum, and diamonds.

carbon dioxide: a gas formed by the burning of fossil fuels, the rotting of plants and animals, and the breathing out of animals, including humans.

carnivore: an animal that eats only other animals.

cell: the most basic part of a living thing. Billions of cells make up a plant or animal, while other organisms are single-celled.

cell wall: the part of a plant cell that gives shape to the cell.

chemical reaction: the change of a substance into a new substance.

chlorophyll: the chemical in a plant's cell that gives a plant its green color.

chloroplast: the part of a plant cell in which sunlight is converted to energy.

chromosome: the part of a cell that contains genes.

climate change: the long-term change in temperature and weather patterns across a large area, in particular a change apparent from the mid-to-late twentieth century onward that has been strongly attributed to the use of fossil fuels as an energy source.

compound microscope: a microscope with two or more lenses.

constrict: to become smaller.

consumer: an organism that eats other organisms.

contaminate: to pollute or make dirty.

convert: to change.

cotyledon: the first leaves produced by a seed.

cross-pollination: the transfer of pollen from one plant to the stigma of another plant.

crustacean: a type of animal, such as a crab or lobster, that lives mainly in water. It has several pairs of legs and its body is made up of sections covered in a hard outer shell.

cyanobacteria: bacteria that use photosynthesis, better known as blue-green algae.

cytoplasm: the gel-like fluid inside a cell.

debris: pieces of dead plants or branches.

decomposer: organisms such as ants, fungi, and worms that break down waste, dead plants, and animals.

defense mechanism: a way to protect oneself.

digest: to break down food that is eaten.

dissect: to cut something apart to study what's inside.

diversity: a range of different things.

DNA: deoxyribonucleic acid. The substance found in your cells that carries your genes, the genetic information that contains the blueprint of who you are.

dormant: in a state of rest or inactivity.

drought: a long period of unusually low rainfall that can harm plants and animals.

dust mite: a microscopic insect that feeds on dead skin cells. Dust mites are a common cause of allergies.

ecosystem: a community of living and nonliving things and their environments.

Egyptologist: a person who studies the history and culture of ancient Egypt.

electron microscope: a type of microscope that uses a beam of electrons to create an image of the specimen.

embryo: a tiny plant inside a seed.

emission: something sent or given off, such as smoke, gas, heat, or light.

endangered: a plant or animal species with a dangerously low population.

endoplasmic reticulum: a network of membranes that makes changes and transports materials through a cell.

environment: everything in nature, living and nonliving, including animals, plants, rocks, soil, and water.

esophagus: the long tube connecting the mouth to the stomach.

evolve: to change or develop gradually.

extinction: the disappearance of a species from the world.

fatal: leading to death.

fermentation: a chemical reaction that breaks down food.

fertile: describes soil that is good for growing crops.

fertilizer: any substance put on land to help crops grow better.

fertilize: to join female and male cells to produce seeds and offspring.

filament: the stalk that supports the anther in a flower.

fission: the splitting of a single-celled organism into two parts.

flammable: something that burns very easily.

fluorescent: a bright color that seems to reflect light.

food chain: a community of animals and plants where each is eaten by another higher up in the chain. Food chains combine into food webs.

fossil fuel: a fuel made from the remains of plants and animals that lived millions of years ago. Coal, oil, and natural gas are fossil fuels.

fungi: plant-like organisms without leaves or flowers that grow on plants and things that are rotting, such as old logs. Examples are mold, mildew, and mushrooms. Singular is fungus.

genes: the basic units in our cells that carry traits and characteristics from one generation to the next.

genetic basis: genes that are beneficial for offspring to inherit.

geotropism: plant growth in response to the force of gravity, which makes the roots grow downwards.

germinate: to sprout and begin to grow.

glacier: an enormous mass of frozen snow and ice that moves across the earth's surface.

glucose: the simple sugar that plants produce through photosynthesis.

Golgi bodies: sacs that receive proteins from the cell, put them together with other proteins, and send them around the cell.

gravity: a force that pulls all objects to Earth.

habitat: the natural area where a plant or animal lives.

herbivore: an animal that eats only plants.

herpetologist: a scientist who studies reptiles and amphibians.

hibernate: to sleep through the winter in a cave or underground.

hormone: a chemical in a plant that controls functions such as plant growth and fruit ripening.

ichthyologist: a scientist who studies fish.

immune system: the system that protects the body against disease and infection.

immunization: making a person or animal immune to infectious disease.

incubate: to develop.

indigenous: native people who originally settled a region; also known as First Nation or First Peoples.

infectious: able to spread quickly from one person to others.

instinct: an inborn behavior, need, or characteristic.

Inupiaq: a group of Alaska Natives whose territory spreads from Norton Sound on the Bering Sea to northern areas of the U.S.-Canada border. They are members of the larger Inuit culture.

invasive species: a species that is not native to an ecosystem and that rapidly expands to crowd out other species.

krill: small crustaceans found in all the world's oceans.

larva: the worm-like stage of an insect's life. Plural is larvae.

lichen: a plant-like organism made of algae and fungus that grows on solid surfaces such as rocks or trees.

life cycle: the growth and changes a living thing goes through, from birth to death.

lysosome: an organelle that aids in digestion.

mammal: an animal such as a human, dog, or cat. Mammals are born live, feed milk to their young, and usually have hair or fur.

marine biology: the study of life in the water.

marine: having to do with the ocean.

membrane: the outer layer of a cell that allows materials to pass in and out.

mesmerize: to hold the attention of a person or people (or an animal) as if in a trance.

metamorphosis: an animal's complete change in physical form as it develops into an adult.

microbe: a tiny living or nonliving thing. Bacteria and fungi are living microbes that are also called microorganisms.

microbiology: the study of microorganisms.

microbiome: a community of microorganisms.

microorganism: a living thing so small that it can be seen only with a microscope.

microscopic: something so small it can be seen only under a microscope.

migration: the seasonal movement of animals from one place to another.

mitochondria: the parts of a cell that change food into energy.

molecules: the tiny particles that make up everything.

multicellular: made up of many cells.

natural selection: one of the basic means of evolution in which organisms that are well-adapted to their environment are better able to survive, reproduce, and pass along their useful traits to offspring.

nectar: a sweet fluid made by flowers that attracts insects.

nucleus: the central part of a cell.

nutrients: substances in food, soil, and air that living things need to live and grow.

offspring: an animal's young.

omnivore: an animal that eats both plants and animals.

organ: a body part that has a certain function, such as the heart or kidneys.

organelle: a structure inside a cell that performs a special function or job.

organic: something that is or was living, such as animals, wood, grass, and insects.

organism: any living thing.

organ system: a group of organs in a living body that work together to do a specific job.

ovary: the part of the pistil in a flower that bears ovules and ripens into a fruit.

overwinter: to last through the winter.

oviparous: an animal that lays eggs.

ovule: a small structure that develops into a seed after it joins with a grain of pollen.

pesticide: a chemical used to kill pests such as insects.

petals: the showy, brightly colored outer area of a flower.

phloem: the structures within plants that bring sugar made during photosynthesis to different parts of the plant.

photosynthesis: the process by which plants produce food, using light as energy.

phototropism: plant growth in response to light, which makes the leaves grow or bend toward a light source.

pigment: a substance that gives something its color.

pioneer: to be one of the first to discover something new.

pistil: the female, seed-producing reproductive part of a flower. It includes the ovary, style, and stigma.

plankton: microscopic plants and animals that float or drift in great numbers in bodies of water.

plaque: a sticky substance that forms on teeth and gums and causes decay.

plumule: the part of a plant embryo that forms a shoot.

pollen: a fine, yellow powder produced by flowering plants. Pollen fertilizes the seeds of other plants as it gets spread around by the wind, birds, and insects.

pollination: the process of transferring male pollen to the female stigma.

pollinator: an insect or other animal that transfers pollen from the male part of a flower to the female part of a flower.

pollutant: something that creates pollution and harms the environment or an ecosystem.

pore: a tiny opening through which substances pass.

precipitation: water in the air in any form, such as snow, hail, or rain, that falls to the ground.

predator: an animal that hunts another animal for food.

prey: an animal hunted and eaten by other animals.

probiotics: microorganisms consumed in foods such as yogurt or miso to keep healthy bacteria in the digestive tract.

proboscis: the sucking mouth part of honeybees and some other insects.

producer: an organism that makes its own food.

projectile vomit: a sudden and strong barfing that causes the vomit to travel some distance.

proteins: substances found in all plants and animals that provide the major structural and functional components of cells.

protoplasm: the colorless liquid that forms the living matter of a cell.

protozoa: microscopic, one-celled organisms. Singular is protozoon.

pseudopod: a foot-like bulge an amoeba uses to move.

radicle: the first part of a plant embryo that emerges and forms a root.

radiograph: an image produced by X-rays or other forms of radiation.

regurgitate: to throw up partially digested food to feed a baby.

remote: faraway and isolated.

reproduce: to make something new just like itself. To have babies.

reptile: a cold-blooded animal such as a snake, lizard, alligator, or turtle that has a spine, lays eggs, has scales or horny places, and breathes air.

resistant bacteria: bacteria that cannot be killed with antibiotics.

revolutionize: to transform, or make a huge and complete change.

ribosome: the protein builder in a cell.

ritual: an action performed in a certain way.

root: the underground plant structure that anchors the plant and takes in water and minerals from soil.

rutting season: the mating time of some animals.

scavenger: an animal, bird, or insect that eats rotting food or animals that are already dead.

seed coat: the hard, protective covering on a seed.

seed: the part of a plant that holds all the beginnings of a plant.

self-pollination: the transfer of a plant's pollen onto its own stigma.

sepals: the special leaves that enclose a flower.

sexual reproduction: reproduction that joins male and female cells.

silt: particles of fine soil, rich in nutrients.

species: a group of plants or animals that are closely related and produce offspring.

specimen: a sample of something.

sperm: the cell that comes from a male in the reproductive process.

spore: a structure produced by fungi that sprouts and grows into a new fungus.

stamen: the male, pollen-producing reproductive part of a flower. It includes the filament and anther.

stem: the plant structure that supports leaves, flowers, and fruits.

stigma: the upper part of the pistil, which receives pollen.

stimulus: a change in an organism's environment that causes an action, activity, or response.

stockpile: to store large amounts of something for later use. Also called hoarding.

stomata: tiny pores on the outside of leaves that allow gases and water vapor to pass in and out.

style: the stalk-like tube that extends from the ovary in a flower to support the stigma.

symbiosis: a relationship between two different species of organisms in which each benefits from the other.

talon: a claw belonging to a bird of prey.

thigmotropism: the response of a plant to physical contact.

tissue: a group or mass of similar cells working together to perform common functions in plants and animals.

topsoil: the top layer of soil.

toxic: poisonous.

toxin: a poisonous or harmful substance.

trait: a characteristic.

translocation: movement of water, sugar, and minerals through a plant.

transpiration: the process by which plants give off water vapor and waste products.

tropism: a plant's involuntary response to a change in its environment.

tsunami: a very large ocean wave, usually caused by an earthquake.

tundra: a treeless Arctic region that is permanently frozen below the top layer of soil.

unicellular: made of only one cell.

vaccine: a substance made up of dead or weakened organisms that, when injected, causes an animal to produce antibodies that protect from the disease caused by those organisms.

vacuole: a compartment in the cytoplasm of a plant cell that stores food and waste.

venomous: poisonous.

ventilate: to supply fresh air into a room or enclosed place.

virologist: a scientist who studies viruses.

virus: a non-living microbe that can cause disease. It can only spread inside the living cells of an organism.

viviparous: an animal that has live births.

warren: a burrow where rabbits live.

water vapor: the gas form of water.

wildlife: animals, birds, and other things that live wild in nature.

xylem: the tubes in plants through which nutrients travel.

zoology: the study of animals.

Metric Conversions

Use this chart to find the metric equivalents to the English measurements in this book. If you need to know a half measurement, divide by two. If you need to know twice the measurement, multiply by two. How do you find a quarter measurement? How do you find three times the measurement?

English	Metric
1 inch	2.5 centimeters
1 foot	30.5 centimeters
1 yard	0.9 meter
1 mile	1.6 kilometers
1 pound	0.5 kilogram
1 teaspoon	5 milliliters
1 tablespoon	15 milliliters
1 cup	237 milliliters

BOOKS

Brodeur, Keiko. *Small Adventures Journal: A Little Field Guide for Big Discoveries in Nature.* Chronicle Books, 2015.

Ignotofsky, Rachel. *The Wondrous Workings of Planet Earth: Understanding Our World and Its Ecosystems.* Ten Speed Press, 2018.

National Geographic Kids. *Ultimate Explorer Field Guide: Mammals.* National Geographic, 2019.

VIDEOS

I'm Only a Kid, I Can't Do Anything About Climate Change. Right?: *youtube.com/watch?v=PslL9WC-2cQ*

Red-Eyed Tree Frog's Life Cycle: *video.nationalgeographic.com/video/ animals/amphibians-animals/frogs-and-toads/frog_greentree_lifecycle*

PBS Science Trek–Soil: *pbs.org/video/soil-video-short-zfxcrn*

MUSEUMS

Natural History Museum, London: *nhm.ac.uk*

Ontario Science Center: *ontariosciencecentre.ca*

Smithsonian Museum of Natural History: *naturalhistory.si.edu/exhibits*

WEBSITES

Audubon: *audubon.org*

NASA Climate Kids: *climatekids.nasa.gov/climate-change-meaning*

National Institute of General Medical Sciences, Cell Images and Videos: *nigms.nih.gov/science-education/explore-by-type/images-videos-and-more*

Smithsonian's National Zoo and Conservation Biology Institute: *nationalzoo.si.edu/audiences/kids/default.cfm?fonzref=kids.htm*

ESSENTIAL QUESTIONS

Introduction: What characteristics do most living things share?

Chapter 1: How do cells act as life's building blocks?

Chapter 2: How do tiny organisms impact our lives?

Chapter 3: Why are plants essential to life on Earth?

Chapter 4: How do plants reproduce?

Chapter 5: How is adaptation necessary for survival?

Chapter 6: Why is reproduction critical for a species' survival?

Chapter 7: How do our actions impact the environment?

QR CODE GLOSSARY

Page 2: *floridatoday.com/videos/news/local/environment/2018/07/17/ new-shark-species-squalus-clarkae-genies-dogfish/36931201*

Page 14: *youtube.com/watch?v=PsYpngBG394*

Page 17: *smithsonianmag.com/smart-news/there-are- 372-trillion-cells-in-your-body-4941473*

Page 21: *youtube.com/watch?v=J-7WwTZvxOA*

Page 21: *twitter.com/SeamusBlackley/status/1158264819503419392*

Page 24: *fsis.usda.gov/wps/wcm/connect/a87cdc2c-6ddd-49f0- bd1f-393086742e68/Molds_on_Food.pdf?MOD=AJPERES*

Page 29: *huntbotanical.org/admin/uploads/hibd-hooke-micrographia-plates.pdf*

Page 30: *youtube.com/watch?v=yutNM8AIkkk*

Page 33: *users.stlcc.edu/kkiser/History.page.html*

Page 37: *youtube.com/watch?v=irjwX3qgtTg*

Page 39: *youtube.com/watch?v=UjnYJVKysfo*

Page 39: *askabiologist.asu.edu/images/plankton-gallery*

Page 43: *youtube.com/watch?v=dKo5IvvtnWw*

Page 51: *youtube.com/watch?v=trWzDlRvv1M*

Page 53: *nationalgeographic.com/news/2017/08/chile- atacama-desert-wildflower-super-bloom-video-spd*

QR CODE GLOSSARY (CONTINUED)

Page 55: *meatlessmonday.com/about-us*

Page 55: *youtube.com/watch?v=NxqBzrx9yIE*

Page 63: *blog.ucsusa.org/science-blogger/timing-pollinators-and-the-impact-of-climate-changePage 2:*

Page 66: *youtube.com/watch?time_continue=9&v=F3Oj2er-91s*

Page 69: *statepress.com/article/2019/09/asu-lab-unlocking-photosythesis-for-better-future*

Page 72: *youtube.com/watch?time_continue=51&v=y9aR2-7sOjg*

Page 76: *video.nationalgeographic.com/video/worlds-deadliest-ngs/deadliest-stoat*

Page 79: *youtube.com/watch?v=fleP9XxJFPY*

Page 80: *video.nationalgeographic.com/video/weirdest-horned-lizard*

Page 82: *abc.net.au/news/2018-09-23/two-headed-snake-found-in-backyard/10295636*

Page 85: *inaturalist.org/projects/north-american-animal-tracking-database*

Page 87: *youtube.com/watch?v=sj8pFX9SOXE*

Page 90: *youtube.com/watch?v=T11rOkgpRnA*

Page 92: *youtube.com/watch?v=M26ug8MGYlY*

Page 93: *theguardian.com/environment/2017/oct/12/penguin-catastrophe-leads-to-demands-for-protection-in-east-antarctica*

Page 93: *youtube.com/watch?v=JjWTJuIc2AQ*

Page 95: *nestwatch.org/learn/how-to-nestwatch/code-of-conduct*

Page 97: *youtube.com/watch?v=Jl5ONrFHhfE*

Page 100: *youtube.com/watch?v=bYxsoLELIuI*

Page 103: *time.com/person-of-the-year-2019-greta-thunberg*

Page 105: *bbc.com/news/world-asia-35638091*

Page 106: *epa.gov/cleanups/cleanups-where-you-live*

Page 107: *scholar.lib.vt.edu/ejournals/JARS/v62n4/v62n4-keshishian.htm*

Page 110: *nwf.org/nativePlantFinder/plants*

Page 110: *canr.msu.edu/publications/how_to_protect_and_increase_pollinators_in_your_landscape*

INDEX

A

activities
A-mazing! Phototropism in a Shoebox, 70–71
Animal Tracker Plaster Caster, 84–85
Bags O' Bread Mold, 24–25
Collect Pond Samples in Your Own Plankton Net, 38–39
Cool Colors, 56
Edible Cell Model, 22–23
Egg-Centric Eggheads, 72
Fantanimal, 83
Fine-Feathered Friends, 95
Flower-Pounding T-Shirt, 53
Grow Microorganisms in a Winogradsky Column, 40–41
Habitat Observation, 82
Hey, Geotropism, 66–67
Metamorpho-Plate, 96–97
Microorganisms and Seed Speed, 42–43
Now You Don't See It, Now You Do!, 36–37
Nutritious and Delicious Plant Parts Salad, 54–55
Organize a Cleanup!, 106
Plant a Mystery Greenhouse Garden, 11
Plant a Pollinator Garden, 110
Roly-Poly Habitat in a Box, 86–87
Test Butterfly Feeders, 108–109
Wetland Plant Pollution, 107
Yeast Balloon Blow Up, 20–21
You Are My Sunshine, 68–69

adaptations, 3, 4, 51, 73–87, 90, 94
air
carbon dioxide in, 21, 47–50, 55
cells requiring, 17
living things needing, 9
oxygen in, 5, 41, 44, 45, 47, 48–50, 52
plants purifying, 44, 49–50
albatrosses, 101
algae, 15, 44, 48, 52
alligators, 12, 74–75, 79
amoebae, 12–14, 16
animals. See also insects; specific animals
adaptations of, 3, 4, 73–87, 90, 94
carnivorous, 7, 76–78
cells of, 4, 12, 14, 16–19
characteristics of, as living things, 4–5
defense mechanisms of, 76, 78–80, 86
energy for, 4, 6. See also food subentry
food/food chain/food web of, 6–7, 51–52, 76–78, 100
largest, 4
life cycles of, 5, 88–97. See also reproduction subentry
mate attraction/mating rituals of, 90–92
natural selection of, 93–94
predator-prey relationships, 76–78, 79
reproduction of, 4–5, 88–89, 92–94
species of, 2
zoology as study of, 3
antibiotics, 25, 32, 34–35

B

backyards, diversity of, iv–v
bacteria, 12, 14–15, 26, 28, 32, 34–35
badgers, honey, 89
biology
branches of, 3. See also botany; microbiology; zoology
definition of, 2
living things in. See animals; fungi; life and living things; microorganisms; plants
Blackley, Seamus, 21
bluebirds, Eastern, 92
botany, 3. See also plants
Bowman, Richard, 21
butterflies, 63, 81, 96–97, 108–109

C

cacti, 4, 44
carbon dioxide, 21, 47–50, 55
carnivores, 7, 12, 51, 76–78
cells, 4, 12–25
chipmunks, 81
chlorophyll, 19, 24, 48, 52, 56
Clark, Eugenie, 2
climate change, 8, 15, 39, 45, 50, 63, 83, 93, 102–103, 108
consumers, 6
crabs, fiddler, 90
crickets, Mormon, 92–94
cytoplasm, 14, 17

D

Darwin, Charles, 94
decomposers, 7, 33, 86
deer, white-tailed, 76–78
defense mechanisms, 76, 78–80, 86
Dutrochet, Henri, 23

E

eagles, harpy, 95
elk, 6
endoplasmic reticulum, 17–18
energy, 4, 5–6, 17, 19, 33. *See also* food/food chain/food web; sun/sunlight
environmental stewardship
  climate change and, 8, 50, 63, 102–103, 108
  food and, 39, 55, 98–101, 104–105, 108–109
  kids and youth involvement in, 102–105
  opportunities and need for, 98–110
  pollution and trash reduction as, 98–102, 104–107
  respectful exploration and, 10
extinction, 45

F

fireflies, 90–91
fish, 15, 29, 38, 79–80, 100
Fleming, Alexander, 25, 32
food/food chain/food web
  animals in, 6–7, 51–52, 76–78, 100
  cells in, 17–18
  definitions of, 6
  environmental damage and protection of, 39, 55, 98–101, 104–105, 108–109
  fungi in, 7, 24, 33
  microorganism in, 6, 14, 38–39
  plants in, 5–7, 19, 45, 46–49, 51–52, 54–55, 69, 100
fox, Arctic, 74
frogs, 12
fulmar, 78–79
fungi, 7, 20–21, 24–25, 33, 36–37, 52

G

geckos, 3
geotropism, 64, 66–67
Golgi bodies, 17–18
grouse, 90

H

hagfish, 79–80
herbivores, 6
hibernation, 81
Hooke, Robert, 27–29

I

insects, 7, 27, 46, 51, 61, 80, 88–94. *See also* butterflies

J

Jenner, Edward, 32–33

K

Kleopfer, John, 82

L

Leeuwenhoek, Antoni van, 27–31
lichens, 44, 52
life and living things. *See also* animals; fungi; microorganisms; plants
  adaptations of, 3, 4, 51, 73–87, 90, 94
  cells of, 4, 12–25
  characteristics of, 4–5, 45
  diversity of, 2, 44–45
  energy for, 4, 5–6, 17, 19, 33. *See also* food/food chain/food web; sun/sunlight
  life cycles of, 5, 57–72, 88–97. *See also* reproduction
  nonliving things vs., 4, 9
  projects and activities on, 9–10. *See also* activities
  reproduction of, 4–5, 16, 24, 36–37, 58–62, 88–89, 92–94
  species of, 2, 27, 45
  study of, 1–10. *See also* botany; microbiology; zoology
  toolkit for studying, 8
Liittschwager, David, 101
lizards, Texas horned, 80
Love, Serena, 21

M

mate attraction/mating rituals, 90–92
medicines, 25, 32–33, 34–35, 47
membranes, cell, 19
metamorphosis, 96–97
microbiology, 3, 26–43. *See also* microorganisms
Micrographia (Hooke), 28
microorganisms. *See also* specific microorganisms
  cells of, 4, 12–14, 16
  characteristics of, as living things, 4–5
  food/food chain/food web of, 6, 14, 38–39
  microbiology as study of, 3, 26–43
  reproduction of, 16
  species of, 27
microscopes, 27–31, 34–35
Middleton, Susan, 101
migration, 81
Milligan-Myhre, Kat Napaaqtuk, 29
mitochondria, 17, 18
mold, 24–25
moose, 91, 92
moss, 12, 19, 44
mushrooms, 33, 36–37

N

natural selection, 93–94
nonliving things, 4, 9
nuclei, 17, 18

O

omnivores, 7
On the Origin of Species (Darwin), 94
organelles, 17–18, 22
owls, 7, 73
oxygen, 5, 16, 41, 44, 45, 47, 48–50, 52

P

panthers, Florida, 76–78
parakeets, 4, 5
Pasteur, Louis, 34
peacocks, 90
penguins, Adélie, 93
penicillin, 25, 32, 34
photosynthesis, 19, 46–49, 52, 68–69
phototropism, 64–66, 70–71
plankton, 38–39, 100
plants. *See also* specific plants
adaptations of, 4, 51
botany as study of, 3
carnivorous, 12, 51
cells of, 4, 12, 14, 16–19
characteristics of, as living things, 4–5, 45
diversity of, 44–45
energy for, 4, 5–6, 19. *See also* food subentry
food/food chain/food web of, 5–7, 19, 45, 46–49, 51–52, 54–55, 69, 100

life cycles of, 5, 57–72. *See also* reproduction subentry
oxygen and air purification by, 5, 44, 45, 47, 48–50, 52
photosynthesis by, 19, 46–49, 52, 68–69
poisonous, 9
pollination of, 46, 57, 60–61, 63, 110
reproduction of, 4–5, 58–62
seeds of, 5, 6, 42–43, 46, 48, 52, 54, 57–58, 62, 72
species of, 2, 45
structure of, 46–47
tropism affecting, 64–67, 70–71
poisonous organisms, 9, 33, 80, 82
pollination, 46, 57, 60–61, 63, 110
pollution/pollution control, 98–102, 104–107
predator-prey relationships, 76–78, 79
producers, 6
proteins, 18–19, 23
protozoa, 28

R

reproduction, 4–5, 16, 24, 36–37, 58–62, 88–89, 92–94
ribosomes, 17–18
Roux, Pierre Paul Émile, 34
rutting season, 92

S

Salk, Jonas, 33
seeds, 5, 6, 42–43, 46, 48, 52, 54, 57–58, 62, 72
sharks, 2, 7, 79–80, 100
sloths, 83
snakes, 74, 82
soil, 9, 11, 40, 42–43, 48, 54–55
spores, 24, 36–37
stoats, 76
Stumpf, Richard P., 15
sun/sunlight, 5–6, 19, 45, 47–49, 64–66, 68–71
symbiosis, 52

T

thigmotropism, 65, 66–67
Thunberg, Greta, 102–103
trash/trash reduction, 98–102, 104–107
trees, redwood, 44
tropism, 64–67, 70–71
turtles, 7, 75, 100

V

vaccines, 32–33, 34
Venus flytraps, 12, 51

W

water, 9, 46–49, 107
whales, 4
Whiting, Evan, 79
Winogradsky, Sergei/ Winogradsky column, 40–41
woodlice, 78, 86–87

Y

yeast, 20–21

Z

zoology, 3. *See also* animals